THE ABC GUIDE TO LONDON

CONTENTS.

ILLUSTRATIONS of Principal Buildings, etc., appear throughout the Book.

THE ROYAL FAMILY	Pages 3 to 7.
The POPULATION OF LONDON, etc., Census Statistics	Pages 15 to 17.
CHRONICLE OF PUBLIC EVENTS, from Queen Victoria's Accession to present time	Pages 27 to 29.
THE A B C GUIDE TO LONDON, with description of all the Places of Interest and Amusement, etc., alphabetically arranged	Pages 31 to 98.
SECTIONAL MAPS OF LONDON	Pages 99 to 114.

Published in Great Britain in 2012 by Old House books & maps,
Midland House, West Way, Botley, Oxford OX2 0PH, United Kingdom.
44-02 23rd Street, Suite 219, Long Island City, NY 11101, USA.
Website: www.oldhousebooks.co.uk
© 2012 Old House.

Every attempt has been made by the Publishers to secure the appropriate
permissions for materials reproduced in this book. If there has been any
oversight we will be happy to rectify the situation and a written submission
should be made to the Publishers.

A CIP catalogue record for this book is available from the British Library.

ISBN-13: 978 1 90840 210 3

Originally published in 1905 by Charles Hooper & Co.,
Alderman's Walk, London.

Printed in China through Worldprint Ltd.

12 13 14 15 16   10 9 8 7 6 5 4 3 2 1

HIS MAJESTY KING EDWARD VII.

OF THE UNITED KINGDOM OF GREAT BRITAIN
AND IRELAND, AND OF ALL THE BRITISH
DOMINIONS BEYOND THE SEAS,
DEFENDER OF THE FAITH, EMPEROR OF INDIA,

Is the Eldest Son of

HER LATE MAJESTY QUEEN VICTORIA

and of

HIS LATE ROYAL HIGHNESS ALBERT PRINCE CONSORT

Was born at Buckingham Palace on the 9th of November, 1841,
and Succeeded to the Throne on the
22nd January, 1901;
Married on the 10th March, 1863, Princess Alexandra,
the eldest daughter of King Christian IX of
Denmark, now

QUEEN ALEXANDRA,

Who was born on December 1st, 1844.

B

Photo by Gunn & Stuart

4

Photo by Gunn & Stuart

THE ROYAL FAMILY—*continued.*

THEIR MAJESTIES' SONS, DAUGHTERS, AND GRANDCHILDREN.

H.R.H. ALBERT VICTOR CHRISTIAN EDWARD, DUKE OF CLARENCE AND AVON DALE, K.G., born January 8th, 1864; died January 14th, 1892.

H.R.H. GEORGE FREDERICK ERNEST ALBERT, K.G., **THE PRINCE OF WALES**, born June 3rd, 1865, Married July 6th, 1893, to H.R.H. PRINCESS VICTORIA MARY OF TECK, **THE PRINCESS OF WALES**, who have had issue:

> EDWARD (THE HEIR PRESUMPTIVE), born June 23rd, 1894.
> ALBERT, born December 14th, 1895.
> VICTORIA ALEXANDRA, born April 25th, 1897.
> HENRY WILLIAM FREDERICK ALBERT, born March 31st, 1900.
> GEORGE EDWARD ALEXANDER EDMUND, born January, 1923.

H.R.H. THE PRINCESS LOUISE, DUCHESS OF FIFE, born February 20th, 1867. Married July 27th, 1889, the Duke of Fife, and has issue:

> Alexandra, born May 17th, 1891.
> Maud, born April 3rd, 1893.

H.R.H. THE PRINCESS VICTORIA, born July 6th, 1868.

H.R.H. THE PRINCESS MAUD, born November 26th, 1869. Married July 22nd, 1896, to Prince Charles, second son of the Crown Prince of Denmark.

ALEXANDER, born April 6th, 1871; died April 7th, 1871.

OTHER MEMBERS OF THE ROYAL FAMILY.

H.R.H. DUKE OF CONNAUGHT, Arthur William Patrick Albert, the third son of H.M. Queen Victoria, and brother of His Majesty King Edward VII. Married March 13th, 1879, Princess Louise Margaret, daughter of the late Prince Frederick Charles of Prussia, and has issue:

> Margaret, born January 15th, 1882.
> Arthur, born January 13th, 1883.
> Victoria Patricia, born March 17th, 1886.

H.R.H. THE PRINCESS CHRISTIAN (Helena Augusta Victoria), sister of His Majesty King Edward VII., was born May 25th, 1846. Married July 5th, 1866, to H.R.H. Prince Christian of Schleswig-Holstein.

H.R.H. THE DUCHESS OF ARGYLL (Louise Caroline Alberta), born March 18th, 1848, and married March 21st, 1871, to the Marquess of Lorne, now Duke of Argyll.

H.R.H. PRINCESS HENRY OF BATTENBERG (Beatrice Mary Victoria Feodore), born April 14th, 1857. Married July 23rd, 1885, to H.R.H. Prince Henry Maurice of Battenberg, who died January 20th, 1896.

H.I.M. WILLIAM II, German Emperor and King of Prussia, the grandson of Queen Victoria, whose mother (the late lamented EMPRESS FREDERICK) was the Princess Royal of England, as Nephew of KING EDWARD VII, has ties of relationship with this country which must help to bind it closer to his own. His presence, with his eldest son, at Osborne and Windsor at the death and funeral of Queen Victoria will long be remembered in England.

[*Continued on page* 7.

OTHER MEMBERS OF THE ROYAL FAMILY—*continued.*

THE CZARINA OF RUSSIA is a daughter of the lamented Grand Duchess of Hesse, His Majesty's sister, who is always affectionately remembered in England as the PRINCESS ALICE.

THE CZAR OF RUSSIA is also closely connected with the English Court, being the nephew of Her Majesty QUEEN ALEXANDRA.

THE DUCHESS OF SAXE-COBURG GOTHA, the widow of the King's brother, who was previously DUKE OF EDINBURGH (who died July 30th, 1900), was before her marriage the Grand Duchess Marie of Russia, born October 17th, 1853.

THE PRESENT DUKE OF SAXE-COBURG-GOTHA is a nephew of the King, being the son of the late DUKE OF ALBANY, popularly known as Prince Leopold, and was born July 19th, 1884. His mother,

THE DUCHESS OF ALBANY, has been a resident in England until her son's acceptance of the Dukedom of Saxe-Coburg on the death of his uncle in 1900.

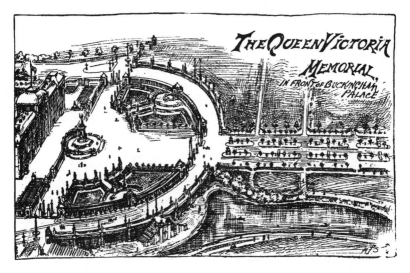

THE NATIONAL MEMORIAL to the late Queen Victoria is proposed to take the form of a statue, by Mr. Brock, outside Buckingham Palace, with a processional avenue stretching through the Mall to Charing Cross, for which the designs of Mr. Aston Webb have been accepted.

FITZ-STEPHEN, 1170 A.D.

" The City of London, like Rome, is divided into wards, has annual sheriffs for its consuls, has senatorial and lower magistrates ; sewers and aqueducts in its streets, its proper places and separate courts for cases of each kind, deliberative, demonstrative, judicial ; and has assemblies on appointed days.

" I do not think there is a city with more commendable customs of church attendance, honour to God's ordinances, keeping sacred festivals, almsgiving, hospitality, confirming betrothals, contracting marriages, celebration of nuptials, preparing feasts, cheering the guests, and also in care for funerals and the interment of the dead. The only pests of London are the immoderate drinking of fools and the frequency of fires. To this it may be added, that nearly all the bishops, abbots, and magnates of England are, as it were, citizens and freemen of London, having their own splendid houses to which they resort, where they spend largely when summoned to great councils by the King, or by their Metropolitan ; or drawn thither by their own private affairs."

BESANT, 1890 A.D.

" London has always been a city looking forwards, pressing forwards, fighting for the future, using up the present ruthlessly for the sake of the future, trampling on the past.

" As it has been so it is. The City may have reached its highest point, it may be about to decline ; but as yet it shows no sign—it has sounded no note of decay, or of decline, or of growing age.

" The City, which began with the East Saxon Settlement among the forsaken streets thirteen hundred years ago, is still in the full strength and lustihood of manhood—perhaps as yet it is only early manhood—for which, as in private duty bound, let us laud, praise, and magnify the providence which has so guided the steps of the citizens and so filled their hearts from generation to generation with the spirit of self-reliance, hope, and courage."

BUCKINGHAM PALACE.

THE KING'S LONDON RESIDENCE.—Stands on the site of Buckingham House, built in 1703 by Sheffield, Duke of Buckingham, George III acquired the site, and Nash rebuilt the palace for George IV in 1825. The east front, facing St. James's Park, was added in 1846 under the supervision of Prince Albert.

THE ROYAL EXCHANGE AND BANK OF ENGLAND.

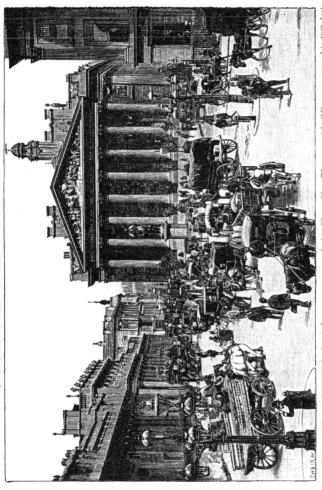

THE ROYAL EXCHANGE is situated on an open space facing Cheapside. The present building was opened in 1845, but the first Exchange on the same spot was opened by Queen Elizabeth in 1579. The present structure encloses a large covered courtyard (with a statue of Queen Victoria in the centre), which is used by merchants to transact business and fix the rate of exchange, etc.

THE BANK OF ENGLAND, the large building on the left of the Exchange, in Threadneedle Street, occupies about three acres of ground. The Bank receives the taxes on behalf of the Government, pays the interest on the National Debt, and issues the well-known Bank of England notes, the value of which in circulation amounts to at least £25,000,000.—*From a Photograph by the London Stereoscopic Company, 54, Cheapside.*

13

LONDON : POPULATION, Etc.

L ONDON, the Capital of Great Britain, is the largest and wealthiest city in the world. It is situated on both sides of the river Thames, about fifty miles from the sea, in latitude 51° 31′N. and longitude 0° 6′ W. from the Royal Observatory, Greenwich. It is supposed to have originated as a small fishing village 2000 years ago, its name being of Celtic derivation—Llyn-din, the fort of the lake or pool. During the Roman occupation it became a considerable trading centre. Roman London, or Augusta, as it was then called, extended for about a mile along the northern bank of the Thames, and was about half-a-mile in breadth. The wall enclosing the City and marking its extent was built about 360 A.D., and some remains are visible to this day in the Churchyard of St. Giles, Cripplegate, and one or two other places. The names of the ancient gates—Aldgate, Bishopsgate, Ludgate, etc., indicate its course.

After the departure of the Romans in 410, the City is supposed to have been deserted for a period, owing to the depredations of invaders. It was not until the beginning of the seventh century that, the country becoming more settled and the City being reoccupied by the Saxons, prosperity began to return.

Alfred the Great made it his capital, instead of Winchester. Edward the Confessor rebuilt the Abbey of Westminster, and William the Conqueror, the builder of the Tower, granted a Charter to the inhabitants.

The foundation of the City Companies gave a great impetus to trade. Progress from that time was rapid, interrupted only by visitations of plague and fire, the curses of mediæval London. What the City was like in those remote times and how the citizens lived are vividly depicted by Sir Walter Besant in his "History of London."

Later, the story of the City is merged in the history of the country. In the record of its growth, it is interesting to recall that edicts were issued by Queen Elizabeth and James I forbidding any further expansion!

At the beginning of a new century it is not uninteresting to compare London of to-day with the London of 1800. In 1800 there were no railways, no cabs, no omnibuses, no telegrams, no telephones, no gas, no electric light, no penny post, and no Metropolitan Police. Now, London is a network of railways, and hardly a month passes without some suggestion for some new tunnelling, and omnibuses are so numerous that it is actually proposed that the Home Secretary should bring a Bill into Parliament to regulate their routes and limit their numbers ; yet the first locomotive, which was constructed by Stephenson, and attained a speed of 6 miles an hour, was not built until 1814, and the first omnibus did not run in England until July 4th, 1829. But we can see the difference still more if we think that our crowded suburbs, from which we go up to work every day, were little country villages, and if we look for the bridges and streets to which, in this year of grace, we are accustomed. A London Bridge, of course, existed in 1800, but not the bridge we know now, which is not on quite the same site as the former one, and was opened in 1831. The only other bridges in existence then were Old Westminster, which was opened in 1750, and Old Blackfriars, which was opened in 1769. The chief of the other bridges were opened as follows :—Vauxhall Bridge, 1816 ; Waterloo B ridge, 1817 ; Southwark Bridge, 1819 ; Hungerford Bridge, 1845 ; Chelsea Bridge, 1858 ; and Tower Bridge, 1894 ; so that in 1800 good people who wished to cross the river had to tramp some way for the means of doing so, or employ the jolly young waterman, who now has entirely disappeared, unless the bargee can be said to be his descendant. Next, take one of our streets, which is perhaps nowadays used more than any other. Regent Street was not in existence in 1800 ; it was not commenced until 1813. Of places of amusement Cremorne and Vauxhall have gone, though Drury Lane and Covent Garden, both rebuilt after destruction by fire, still exist. The Haymarket existed in 1800, as did the Lyceum, under the name of the English Opera House. The Adelphi was not opened until 1806, the St. James's until 1835, the Princess's until 1840. Astley's, which was open in 1800, has gone. The Surrey was in existence, but our other theatres are of later date, excepting old Sadler's Wells. Music-halls in 1800 were unknown, so perhaps one of the greatest contrasts between London past and London present is to be found in our amusements.

The following table of population at various periods will show the enormous growth of the nineteenth century, in comparison with the previous 1800 years, and will most clearly indicate the stimulating effect of the great inventions and discoveries of the Victorian Era :—

THE POPULATION OF LONDON.						
In the year 1066, William the Conqueror's time,	}	was about	40,000			
In the year 1700	...	...	,,	700,000		
,, ,, 1801	...	... by Census	958,863			
,, ,, 1821	...	...	,,	1,378,947		
,, ,, 1841	...	...	,,	1,918,417		
,, ,, 1861	...	...	,,	2,803,989		
,, ,, 1881	...	...	,,	3,815,544	or Greater London,	4,776,661
,, ,, 1891	...	...	,,	4,211,056	,, ,,	5,633,332
,, ,, 1901	...	...	,,	4,536,541	,, ,,	6,581,372

What is called GREATER LONDON is the area included in the Metropolitan and City of London Police districts, and comprises an area close upon 700 square miles, containing over 800,000 inhabited houses, and a population of 6,581,372.

NOTE.

The figures given for the Metropolitan Boroughs, which have only recently come into existence, show the population of each Borough in 1901, and also the population within the present boundaries of these Boroughs enumerated in 1891.

POPULATION in 1891 AND 1901 IN THE CITY OF LONDON AND THE METROPOLITAN BOROUGHS **within the County of London.**

	Population.	
	1891.	1901.
City of London	37,702 ...	26,923
Battersea	150,166 ...	168,907
Bermondsey	136,014 ...	130,760
Bethnal Green	128,929 ...	129,680
Camberwell	233,706 ...	259,339
Chelsea	72,954 ...	73,842
Deptford	101,770 ...	110,398
Finsbury	109,981 ...	101,463
Fulham	91,790 ...	137,289
Greenwich	78,493 ...	95,770
Hackney	199,606 ...	219,272
Hammersmith	97,283 ...	112,239
Hampstead	68,126 ...	81,942
Holborn	66,781 ...	59,405
Islington	319,155 ...	334,991
Kensington	170,071 ...	176,628
Lambeth	278,393 ...	301,895
Lewisham	88,933 ...	127,495
Paddington	135,955 ...	143,976
Poplar	166,880 ...	168,822
St. Marylebone	144,083 ...	133,301
St. Pancras	234,748 ...	235,317
Shoreditch	124,727 ...	118,637
Southwark	202,479 ...	206,180
Stepney	285,116 ...	298,600
Stoke Newington	47,988 ...	51,247
Wandsworth	155,524 ...	232,034
Westminster, City of	201,969 ...	183,011
Woolwich	98,994 ...	117,178
Administrative County of London	4,228,317 ...	4,536,541

There were at the last Census 4,189,732 English people in London. Of these, 3,016,580 were natives of London, leaving 1,173,152 English persons who, born in the country, had made London their residence.

English	4,189,732	⎫
Scotch	56,605	⎪ Making the complete total
Irish	60,211	⎪ of residents in the Ad-
Welsh	35,421	⎬ ministrative County of
British Colonies and Dependencies	33,350	⎪ London, at the Census
British subjects and naturalised British subjects ...	25,845	⎪ of 1901, 4,536,541.
*Number of people from foreign countries in London	135,377	⎭

* *Amongst these are 27,427 Germans, 11,264 French, 38,117 Russians, 15,420 Russian Poles, and 10,889 Italians.*

There are over a million families or separate occupiers in London. The males number 2,142,085, and the females 2,394,456. The number of domestic servants in London is 249,823. *(These figures are for London within the Administrative County only.)*

The following are the Census Returns for the largest Cities and Boroughs in the United Kingdom:—

	1891.	1901.		1891.	1901.		1891.	1901.
LONDON ...	4,211,056	4,536,541	Belfast ...	255,896	348,965	Nottingham	213,877	239,753
Glasgow ...	564,968	735,906	Bristol ...	289,280	328,842	Salford ...	198,139	220,956
Liverpool ...	629,548	684,947	Edinburgh..	261,261	316,479	Newcastle-on-		
Manchester	505,368	543,969	Dublin ...	278,896	289,108	Tyne ...	186,300	214,803
Birmingham	478,113	522,182	Bradford ...	265,728	279,809	Leicester ...	174,624	211,574
Leeds ...	367,505	428,953	West Ham..	204,903	267,308			
Sheffield ...	324,243	380,717	Hull... ...	200,472	240,618			

VIEW OF THE WEST FRONT OF WESTMINSTER ABBEY.

WESTMINSTER ABBEY, founded by King Edward the Confessor, about 1055-65, on the site of a still more ancient church, was rebuilt in the thirteenth century by Henry III and his son, Edward I; the Chapel of Henry VII was erected in the sixteenth century; and the towers were completed in 1714. Most of the English kings and queens have been crowned in this grand old building. It is also the burial-place of many kings, queens, celebrated men, etc.

19

THE CHOIR OF WESTMINSTER ABBEY.

The following are the Kings and Queens who have been crowned here:—

WILLIAM THE CONQUEROR, 1066.

WILLIAM RUFUS, 1087.

HENRY I, 1100.

STEPHEN, 1135.

HENRY II, 1154.

RICHARD CŒUR DE LION, 1189.

JOHN, 1199.

HENRY III., 1220.

EDWARD I., 1274.

EDWARD II., 1308.

RICHARD II., 1377.

HENRY IV., 1399.

HENRY V., 1413.

HENRY VII., 1429.

EDWARD IV., 1461.

RICHARD III., 1483.

HENRY VII., 1485.

HENRY VIII., 1509.

EDWARD VI. 1547.

MARY, 1553.

ELIZABETH, 1559.

JAMES I., 1603.

CHARLES I., 1626.

CHARLES II., 1661.

JAMES II., 1685.

WILLIAM & MARY I., 1689.

ANNE, 1702.

GEORGE I., 1714.

GEORGE II., 1727.

GEORGE III., 1761.

GEORGE IV., 1821.

WILLIAM IV., 1831.

VICTORIA, 1838.

WHERE THE KINGS AND QUEENS OF ENGLAND ARE CROWNED IN STATE,

And where the Coronation of KING EDWARD VII and QUEEN ALEXANDRA took place on August 9, 1902.

NATURAL HISTORY MUSEUM. A noble building in the Romanesque style. Designed by Mr. Alfred Waterhouse. Begun in 1873 and completed in 1880. The extreme length of the front is 675 feet. The great hall is 170 feet long by 97 feet wide. Contains the Natural History collection formerly in the British Museum at Bloomsbury.

The following is a List of some of the

SPECIAL PLACES OF INTEREST
AND ENTERTAINMENT FOR LONDON VISITORS, ETC.

THE TOWER.—Open from 10 to 6. Mondays and Saturdays, free; other days, 1s.; *See pages 87 and 88.*

WESTMINSTER ABBEY.—Open free daily to the Services. On Mondays, Tuesdays, and Wednesdays, Henry VII.'s and the smaller Chapels are also open free; on other days, 6d. For further particulars, *see page 94, etc.*

BRITISH MUSEUM.—From 10 a.m. until 6. Closed earlier in Winter. *See page 38.*

VICTORIA & ALBERT MUSEUM.—SOUTH KENSINGTON. On Mondays, Tuesdays, and Saturdays, from 10 to 10. Free. Other days, 10 to 4 or 6, 6d. On Sundays the whole of the Museum (excepting the Libraries) is open free from 2 p.m. till dusk. *See pages 50, 51, and 72.*

NATURAL HISTORY MUSEUM.—SOUTH KENSINGTON. From 10 a.m. until 6. Free. *See pages 22 and 72.*

NATIONAL GALLERY.—On Mondays, Tuesdays, Wednesdays, and Saturdays, from 10 till dusk. Free. Thursdays and Fridays, 10 till 5, 6d. On Sundays from 2 till 4 p.m. *See page 72.*

THE NATIONAL GALLERY OF BRITISH ART (known as the Tate Gallery).—GROSVENOR ROAD, S.W. Open Free on Mondays, Thursdays, Fridays, and Saturdays, from 10 to 4 in Winter, 10 to 6 in Summer, and on Sundays from 2 to 6, in Winter from 2 till dusk.

THE WALLACE COLLECTION, HERTFORD HOUSE.—MANCHESTER SQUARE, W. Open free on Mondays, Wednesdays, Thursdays, and Saturdays. On Tuesdays and Fridays, 11 to 6, 6d.: Sundays in Summer from 2 to 6. *See pages 92 and 93.*

ST. PAUL'S CATHEDRAL.—Between the Services, for small fees, the public can visit the Crypt, also the Whispering Gallery, and the Ball on top of the Dome. *See page 80.*

UNITED SERVICE MUSEUM.—WHITEHALL. An interesting collection of weapons, models, and relics. Open from 11 to 6 in Summer; 11 to 4 in Winter. Admission, 6d. *See pages 72 and 8*.

GREENWICH HOSPITAL AND NAVAL MUSEUM.—Open to the Public free every day except Friday, from 10 to 4 or 6, also (excepting the Museum) on Sundays from 2 o'clock. For further particulars *see page 60.*

HAMPTON COURT PALACE.—Open free every day except Friday, from 10 to 4 or 6; Sundays from 2 p.m. For further particulars, *see page 60.*

KEW GARDENS.—Open daily, 12 till 6; also on Sundays at 1. Free. *See page 66.*

HYDE PARK AND KENSINGTON GARDENS.—For the Albert Memorial and Kensington Palace, *see pages 65 and 66.*

KENSINGTON PALACE is open to the public free every week-day, excepting Wednesday, from 10 to 4 or 6; Sundays open at 2. *See page 66.*

ZOOLOGICAL GARDENS.—Situated in Regent's Park. Admission, 1s.; Mondays, 6d.; children always 6d. For further particulars, *see pages 97 and 98.*

THE MONUMENT.—View from the top. 3d. each. From 9 to 4 daily. *See page 71.*

THE IMPERIAL INSTITUTE.—SOUTH KENSINGTON. Open daily, except Sunday, from 11 a.m. to 10 p.m. Admission free. *See page 65.*

CRYSTAL PALACE.—Daily. Admission usually, 1s. For entertainments see daily papers.

MADAME TUSSAUD'S WAXWORKS.—Close to Baker Street Station. Open daily Admission, 1s.

HOUSES OF PARLIAMENT.—*See page 63.*

ST. JAMES'S PARK.—To see the Horse Guards and Buckingham Palace.

COVENT GARDEN MARKET.—For Fruit, Flowers, etc. Strand.

TEMPLE CHURCH.—Services on Sunday at 11. This is the old Knights Templar Church. Oliver Goldsmith was buried here. *See page 85.*

FOUNDLING CHAPEL, Foundling Hospital, Guildford Street.—No visitor to London should miss attending service in the Chapel at 11 a.m. on Sundays; the singing by the children, assisted by distinguished professionals, is most beautiful. Some valuable pictures by Hogarth, etc., curiosities, etc., can be seen after the service. *See page 56.*

For Particulars of Exhibitions, Theatres, Concerts, Music Halls, etc., see Daily Papers.

WINDSOR CASTLE.

WINDSOR CASTLE, the principal residence of the reigning monarch, is situated on the Thames, about 20 miles from London. The State Apartments are open to the public, when the Court is absent, on Monday, Tuesday, Thursday, Friday, and Saturday, from 11 to 4. St. George's Chapel and the Albert Memorial Chapel are also open to visitors. The Great Park extends 6 miles to Virginia Water. Windsor is reached by rail from Paddington (G. W. R.) or Waterloo (L. & S. W. R.). *See page 97.—From a photograph by G. W. Wilson, Aberdeen.*

In Memoriam.

HER LATE MAJESTY QUEEN VICTORIA,

Who Ascended the Throne, June 20th, 1837;
was Crowned in Westminster Abbey, June 28th, 1838;
and Proclaimed Empress of India, January 1st, 1877.

Died January 22nd, 1901.

HAMPTON COURT PALACE.

HAMPTON COURT PALACE, well known as the old Palace of Cardinal Wolsey, and presented by him to Henry VIII., was for many years a royal residence. In the rooms are exhibited a large collection of pictures, etc., many of great historical interest. Beautiful gardens and grounds surround the Palace, which is situated on the banks of the Thames near Kingston. It is open every day but Friday, and is reached by rail from Waterloo Station.

CHRONICLE OF PUBLIC EVENTS
DURING QUEEN VICTORIA'S REIGN AND TO THE PRESENT TIME.

1837. Queen Victoria's Accession to the Throne, June 20th.
1838. The Coronation of Queen Victoria, June 28th. Afghan War. Mails first sent by rail.
1839. Beginning of war with China.
1840. The Marriage of Queen Victoria to Albert, Duke of Saxony, Prince of Coburg and Gotha, February 10th. Penny Post began, January 10th.
1841. King Edward VII. born November 9th. Sir Robert Peel's Administration succeeded Viscount Melbourne's. British occupation of Cabul and insurrection.
1842. British Army returned from Cabul and destroyed in the Khyber Pass. Capture of Cabul. Peace of Nankin, with China.
1843. Scinde War. Annexation of Natal.
1844. Blockade of the Harbour of the Piræus, Queen Victoria opened the Royal Exchange, October 28th.
1845. Anti-Corn Law agitation. Sikh War.
1846. Lord John Russell's Administration succeeded Sir Robert Peel's.
1847. House of Lords met in the new House for the first time, April 15th.
1848. Lord Melbourne died, November 24th.
1849. Annexation of the Punjaub, March 29th.
1850. Death of Sir Robert Peel, July 2nd.
1851. The Great Exhibition opened, May 1st. Burmese War.
1852. Earl of Derby's Administration succeeded Lord John Russell's, and the Earl of Aberdeen's the Earl of Derby's. Death of the Duke of Wellington, September 14th.
1853. Protocol signed between England, France, Austria, and Prussia for the re-establishment of peace between Russia and Turkey, December 5th.
1854. Queen Victoria opened the Crystal Palace, June 10th. War declared against Russia, March 28th. Battles of the Alma, September 20th; Balaclava, October 25th; Inkerman, November 5th.
1855. Viscount Palmerston's Administration succeeded the Earl of Aberdeen's. Peace with Russia proclaimed, April 19th. Queen Victoria distributed Crimean Medals, April 10th.
1856. War with China. Annexation of Oude.
1857. Indian Mutiny began. Victoria Crosses presented by Queen Victoria in Hyde Park, June 26th.
1858. Earl of Derby's Administration succeeded Viscount Palmerston's. The East India Company's political power ceased, September 1st.
1859. Viscount Palmerston's Administration succeeded the Earl of Derby's. Proclamation for the organisation of Volunteer Rifle Corps.
1860. Queen Victoria reviewed 18,450 Volunteers in Hyde Park, June 23rd.
1861. Death of the Prince Consort, December 14th. Death of the Duchess of Kent (the Queen's mother), March 16th. Constitution of the Order of the Star of India, June 25th.
1862. British Burma constituted.
1863. Marriage of King Edward VII. (then Prince of Wales) to Princess Alexandra of Denmark, March 10th.
1864. Albert Memorial begun, May 13th.
1865. Death of Lord Palmerston, October 18th. Earl Russell's Administration.
1866. Earl of Derby's Administration succeeded Earl Russell's. The Atlantic Cable laid.
1867. Abyssinian War.
1868. Capture of Magdala and conclusion of Abyssinian War. Disraeli reconstituted the Administration on the Earl of Derby's resignation from ill health, and was succeeded at the end of the year by Gladstone. Queen Victoria laid the foundation stone of St. Thomas's Hospital, May 13th.
1869. Death of the Earl of Derby. Queen Victoria inaugurated Holborn Viaduct and the New Blackfriars Bridge, November 6th.
1870. New Buildings of the London University inaugurated by Queen Victoria, May 11th.
1871. British Columbia united to the Dominion of Canada. Colony of Griqualand constituted. Royal Albert Hall opened by Queen Victoria, March 29th.
1872. The first election by ballot, Pontefract, August 15th. National thanksgiving for the recovery of the Prince of Wales (now King Edward VII.), February 29th.
1873. Ashantee War.
1874. Disrali's Administration succeeds Gladstone's. Capture of Comassie and end of Ashantee War. Gold Coast Colony formed.
1875. Departure of the Prince of Wales (now King Edward VII.) for India.
1876. Queen Victoria proclaimed Empress of India.
1877. Institution of the Imperial Order of the Crown of India.
1878. Afghan War. Treaty of Berlin signed, July 13th. Earl Russell died, May 28th.
1879. Zulu War.

[Continued on page 29.

ROTTON ROW, HYDE PARK.

ROTTON ROW is the well-known road for equestrians in Hyde Park. It commences at Hyde Park Corner, and is very largely used—especially during the London Season—by the fashionable world. The Carriage Drive is also thronged during the summer afternoons between 4 and 6.

CHRONICLE OF PUBLIC EVENTS—*continued.*

1880. Gladstone's Administration succeeded Disrali's. Final settlement of Afghan troubles.

1881. The Abolition of Flogging by Army Discipline Act, The Earl of Beaconsfield (Disrali) died, April 19th. Transvaal War.

1882. Bombardment of Alexandria, battles of Kassassin and Tel-el-Kebir. Queen Victoria opened the New Law Courts, December 4th.

1883. Parliament Buildings at Quebec burnt, April 19th.

1884. Soudan War.

1885. The Marquis of Salisbury's Administration succeeded Gladstone's. Bechuanaland proclaimed British territory. Burmese War.

1886. Gladstone's Administration succeeded the Marquis of Salisbury's. The Marquis of Salisbury returned to power in July. Zululand added to the Empire, and Annexation of Upper Burmah. Foundation stone of the Examination Hall of the Royal College of Physicians and Surgeons laid by Queen Victoria, March 14th.

1887. CELEBRATION OF QUEEN VICTORIA'S JUBILEE, June 21st. The People's Palace opened by Her Majesty, May 14th.

1888. Silver Wedding of King Edward VII. and his Consort (then Prince and Princess of Wales), March 10th.

1889. Prince of Wales unveiled statue of Queen Victoria in the Royal College of Physicians May 24th.

1890. Mashonaland and Matabeleland added to the Empire. Heligoland ceded to Germany.

1891. Queen Victoria present at the launch of the *Royal Sovereign* and of the *Royal Arthur* at Portsmouth, February 26th.

1892. Gladstone's Administration succeeded the Marquis of Salisbury's.

1893. Imperial Institute inaugurated by Queen Victoria, May 10th.

1894. Earl of Rosebery's Administration after Gladstone's retirement. Queen Victoria inaugurated the Manchester Ship Canal, May 21st.

1895. The Marquis of Salisbury's Administration succeeded the Earl of Rosebery's. Chitral War and occupation of Chitral.

1897. THE DIAMOND JUBILEE OF QUEEN VICTORIA CELEBRATED ON JUNE 22ND THROUGHOUT GREAT BRITAIN AND THE COLONIES.—In London especially by the great procession of Her Majesty to St. Paul's, followed by Illuminations, Free Dinners to the Poor, and other festivities.

1898. Death of Mr. Gladstone. Reconquest of the Soudan.

1899. Queen Victoria laid the first stone of the Victoria and Albert Museum frontage, South Kensington.

1900. War commenced against England by the Boers in the Transvaal and Orange Free State, which at first resulted in the overrunning of Cape Colony and the siege of Ladysmith, Kimberley, and Mafeking. The former were relieved in March, and the latter on May 16th, to the great joy and delight of London and the country, and with great national enthusiasm for the Generals—Roberts, Kitchener, Buller, White, etc., etc.—who had thus successfully carried on a most difficult campaign.

1901. DEATH OF QUEEN VICTORIA, January 22nd. Public Funeral of the QUEEN through London *en route* to Windsor, where she lies buried with her husband, PRINCE ALBERT. Proclamation of KING EDWARD VII. at St. James's Palace and in the City. The King opens his first Parliament. Desultory continuation of the War in South Africa. Lord Kitchener constructing a huge system of blockhouses.

1902. First Court and *Levee* of the KING at Buckingham and St. James's Palaces. Death of Cecil Rhodes, the African Empire-maker, and disposition of his property, by will, for Empire purposes. King of Portugal visited England. Assuan Barrage inaugurated by Duchess of Connaught. The long-drawn-out and expensive war in South Africa terminates. PEACE PROCLAIMED, MAY 31, 1902.
THE CORONATION, fixed for June 26, was postponed on account of the sudden illness of the King. The operation which immediately followed was, happily, successful, and the intense anxiety of his people was relieved by his gradual recovery. This was, fortunately, so complete by August that the Coronation took place on the 9th, shorn, however, of many features of the magnificent ceremonial originally contemplated.
In November the Right Hon. Joseph Chamberlain started on his mission of pacification to the Cape.

1903. Delhi Durbar. Coronation proclaimed in India. King visited Rome. Corn Duty repealed. King visited President Loubet. King and Queen of Servia Assassinated. President Loubet visited London. Pope Leo died, Pius X. appointed. Death of Lord Salisbury. King visited Marienbad and Austria. Honourable Artillery Company's visit to America. Alaska Boundary Dispute settled. Panama Canal Treaty signed.

MEMORIAL TABLETS.

The following is a complete list of the Memorial Tablets which have been erected by the Society of Arts on houses in London associated with distinguished men and women :—

JOANNA BAILLIE, Bolton House, Windmill Hill, Hampstead.

JAMES BARRY, 36, Castle Street, Oxford Street.

ELIZABETH BARRETT BROWNING, 15, Wimpole Street.

ROBERT BROWNING, 19, Warwick Crescent, Paddington.

EDMUND BURKE, 37, Gerrard Street, Soho.

LORD BYRON, 16, Holles Street.

> [The house was pulled down in 1889. In May, 1900, Messrs. John Lewis & Co., Silk Mercers, erected on the front of the new house (now in their occupation) a fre-h memorial, consisting of a bronze relief bust of Byron placed in an architectural frame of Portland Stone.]

GEORGE CANNING, 37, Conduit Street.

GEORGE CRUIKSHANK, 263, Hampstead Road.

MADAME D'ARBLAY (FANNY BURNEY), 11, Bolton Street, Piccadilly.

CHARLES DICKENS, Furnival's Inn.

> [The whole of Furnival's Inn was pulled down in 1898.]

JOHN DRYDEN, 43, Gerrard Street.

MICHAEL FARADAY, 2, Blandford Street, Portman Square.

JOHN FLAXMAN, 7, Buckingham Street, Fitzroy Square.

BENJAMIN FRANKLIN, 7, Craven Street, Strand,

THOMAS GAINSBOROUGH, Schomberg House (now part of the War Office), Pall-Mall.

DAVID GARRICK, 5, Adelphi Terrace.

EDWARD GIBBON, 7, Bentinck Street.

GEORGE FREDERICK HANDEL, 25, Brook Street.

SIR ROWLAND HILL, Bertram House, Hampstead.

WILLIAM HOGARTH, 30, Leicester Square.

JOHN KEATS, Lawnbank, Hampstead.

SAMUEL JOHNSON, 17, Gough Square, Fleet Street.

NAPOLEON III., 3a, King Street, St. James's.

LORD NELSON, 147, New Bond Street.

SIR ISAAC NEWTON, 35, St. Martin's Street.

PETER THE GREAT, 15, Buckingham Street, Strand.

SIR JOSHUA REYNOLDS, 47, Leicester Square.

JOHN RUSKIN, 54, Hunter Street, Brunswick Square.

RICHARD BRINSLEY SHERIDAN, 14, Savile Row.

WM. MAKEPIECE THACKERAY, Kensington Palace Green.

JOHN THURLOE, 24, Old Square, Lincoln's Inn.

SIR HARRY VANE, Belmont, Rosslyn Hill, Hampstead.

SIR ROBERT WALPOLE, 5, Arlington Street.

JOHN MILTON, Bunhill Row.

The following tablets were erected by the London County Council :—

LORD MACAULAY, Holly Lodge, Campden Hill, Kensington, W.

CHARLES DICKENS, 48, Doughty Street, Mecklenburgh Square, W.C.

SIR ROBERT PEEL, 4, Whitehall Gardens.

The A B C GUIDE to LONDON

ACADEMY OF ARTS (THE ROYAL) BURLINGTON HOUSE, PICCADILLY.—Open from first Monday in May to first Monday in August from 8 a.m. to 7 p.m. for the Annual Exhibition of Pictures by living Artists. Admission 1s. During the last week open also from 7.30 p.m. to 10.30 p.m.: admission 6d. The Royal Academicians elect their own members and associates. The President is always an artist of rank, and the position has been lately occupied by Lord Leighton, Sir John Millais. The present President is Sir E. J. Poynter. In addition to the Annual Exhibition there is usually one of works by Old Masters and deceased British Artists for ten weeks, commencing on the first Monday in January from 9 a.m. to 6 p.m.: admission 1s. Gibson and Diploma Galleries, free daily, from 11 a.m. to 4 p.m.

ACADEMY OF MUSIC (THE ROYAL), TENTERDEN STREET, HANOVER SQUARE.— For teaching all kinds of music to advanced pupils.

ACHILLES STATUE, in HYDE PARK, was cast from cannon taken in the Peninsular War, and at Waterloo; was presented by the women of England to the Duke of Wellington.

ACTON.—A western suburb of London, about 5 miles from Charing Cross.

ADDINGTON.—Three miles from Croydon. For many years the residence of the Archbishop of Canterbury.

ADDISCOMBE.—Near Croydon.

ADELPHI (THE).—Comprises three or four streets on south side of Strand.

ADELPHI THEATRE. 411, STRAND.—Nearest Railway Station, Charing Cross.

ADMIRALTY. The Admiralty is in WHITEHALL, with large extensions lately added in the rear overlooking the Horse Guards' Parade and St James's Park.—Here is conducted the official work of the largest Navy in the world. The First Lord of the Admiralty is responsible to Parliament for this department of the State, and is necessarily a prominent member of the Government. Office hours 10 a.m. to 5 p.m. Nearest Railway Station, Charing Cross.

AGRICULTURAL HALL. Near "The Angel," Islington.—The Christmas Cattle Show and different Trade Exhibitions, etc., are held here. Nearest Railway Stations, King's Cross, or Electric Railway from City to "The Angel,"; or by 'Bus and Tram.

ALBANY (THE). Leads from Piccadilly to Burlington Gardens.—A collection of houses let as Chambers. Many years ago the occupiers were known as "Bachelors of the Albany."

ALBEMARLE STREET. Leading out of Piccadilly.—In this street are situated Royal Institution, Royal Thames Yacht Club, Albemarle Club, Royal Asiatic Society, etc.. etc.

ALBERT SUSPENSION BRIDGE crosses the Thames from Chelsea Embankment to Battersea Park; was opened in 1873.

ALBERT BRIDGE. WINDSOR HOME PARK.—Crosses the Thames half a mile below Datchet: It connects Berkshire and Buckinghamshire.

31

ALBERT EMBANKMENT.—Situated on the right bank of the Thames, from a point a little below Vauxhall Bridge to Westminster Bridge, nearly a mile long.

ALBERT HALL. KENSINGTON.—A large round building close to the Albert Memorial. Used principally for Concerts on a large scale. Will hold an audience of 10,000. The Orchestra accommodates 1,000 performers. Nearest Railway Stations, High Street, Kensington and South Kensington.

ALBERT MEMORIAL. HYDE PARK.—Close to Albert Hall. Erected to the memory of the late Prince Consort, at a cost of £120,000. Designed by Sir Gilbert Scott, and consists of a bronzed gilt statue of the Prince Consort by Foley, under a Gothic canopy, and surrounded by groups of statuary representing Europe, Asia, Africa and America, etc., Nearest Railway Station, same as Albert Hall.

ALDERSGATE.—One of the 26 wards of London, called from the old City Gate which stood near the Church of St. Botolph.

ALDERSGATE STREET.—A main entrance to the City; was once famous for old mansions and inns.

ALDGATE, or **OLD GATE,** was the ancient east gate of the City.

ALEXANDRA HOUSE. SOUTH KENSINGTON.—Opened by Queen Alexandra to afford, at a moderate expense, a home for young ladies who come to London for education.

ALEXANDRA PALACE AND PARK. MUSWELL HILL, 6 miles North of London.—Is now open free to the people under the management of Trustees selected from the Middlesex, London and local County Councils. Entertainments of a popular character are provided, and only small fees are charged for the high-class Concerts, Plays, etc., which are constantly being produced here. Fireworks are a feature of the summer season. Picture Gallery, Skating Rink, Water Chute, Boating on the Lake, etc., constitute some of the many forms of entertainment. With cheaper tram fares to and from the Palace it is hoped that this additional free and open space, so beautifully situated, will be more and more appreciated by the immense population of North London. Reached by train (G.N.Ry.) from Moorgate Street and King's Cross, or (N.L.Ry.) from Broad Street *via* Finsbury Park : also (G.E.Ry.) from Liverpool Street *via* Hackney Downs and Seven Sisters Stations, to Palace Gates.

ALHAMBRA. LEICESTER SQUARE.—One of the large houses for Ballet and Variety Entertainments. Admission 1s. to 7s. 6d. Nearest Railway Station, Charing Cross. Doors open 7.45.

AMBULANCE ASSOCIATION. Headquarters, St. John's Gate, Clerkenwell.—This gate is all that remains of the Monastery of the Knights of St. John of Jerusalem, founded in 1100, but destroyed by Wat Tyler in 1382.

AMBULANCE SERVICE (Office, Norfolk House, Norfolk Street, W.C.) provides about fifty ambulance stations in London.

AMEN CORNER. AVE MARIA LANE, PATERNOSTER ROW.—So called from text writers formerly dwelling there.

AMERICAN EMBASSY. 123, Victoria Street, S.W.

AMERICAN CONSULATE. 12, St. Helen's Place, Bishopsgate, E.C.

AMERICAN READING ROOMS.—Gilligs', U.S. Exchange, 9, Strand.

AMUSEMENTS. See under different headings, Theatres, Music Halls, Entertainments.

AMWELL.—A village in Hertfordshire. The New River is supplied from a spring that rises in this place.

ANERLEY.—A suburb on the South Eastern line, near Sydenham, 7½ miles from London.

ANTIQUARIAN SOCIETY.—Founded about 1572. Burlington House.

APOTHECARIES' HALL, WATER LANE, BLACKFRIARS, Is occupied by the Society of Apothecaries of London.

APSLEY HOUSE, at HYDE PARK CORNER, is the residence of the Duke of Wellington. The old Duke lived here from 1820 till 1852. The Duke's bedroom was a narrow, ill-lighted chamber on the eastern side of the house.

AQUARIUM (ROYAL). WESTMINSTER.—Long known as a popular place of entertainment. The whole site has been acquired by the Wesleyans, who propose to make their headquarters there.

WHITEHALL.

THE HORSE GUARDS stands on the site of the old Tilt Yard at Westminster, where tournaments were held in Tudor Times. The Admiralty, Foreign, India, Colonial, and Home Offices are all closely adjoining in Whitehall or immediate vicinity.

33

ARMY AND NAVY PENSIONERS' EMPLOYMENT SOCIETY. CHARING CROSS.—Employers can be supplied with men on application.

ART EXHIBITIONS.—Principally open during the London Season.
Royal Academy, Burlington House, Piccadilly, May to July inclusive. Admission 1s.
Diploma and Gibson Galleries, also at Royal Academy, open daily. Free.
The New Gallery, 121, Regent Street, Summer and Winter Exhibitions. Admission 1s.
Royal Society of Painters in Water Colours, 5A, Pall Mall East. Admission 1s.
Royal Institute of Painters in Water Colours, 191, Piccadilly. Admission 1s.
Society of British Artists, 6½, Suffolk Street, Pall Mall. Admission 1s.
[*See also* PICTURE GALLERIES.]

ARTILLERY COMPANY.—The Honourable Artillery Company of the City of London dates from as far back as 1537. All the Officers of the old City Trained Bands were selected from members of the Company. The Artillery Ground, near Finsbury Square, contains a good Drill Hall. It is the only Volunteer Corps that includes Horse Artillery, and they wear the bearskin head-dress, otherwise peculiar to the Guards.

ART TRAINING SCHOOLS. SOUTH KENSINGTON.—For training of teachers, male and female, in the practice of Art, with a view to qualify them as teachers of Schools of Art, in Freehand, Architectural and Mechanical Drawing, Geometry, Painting in Oil and Water Colours, Modelling, Moulding and Casting. These Courses of instruction are open to the public on payment of fees; the classes for Male and Female Students meeting separately. The Fees are as follows: Fees for Classes studying for five whole days, including evenings, £5 for five months, and an entrance fee of 10s. Evening Classes, Male School, £2 per term, Female School, £1 per term, three evenings a week. Special low terms for Governesses in Private Schools or Families. Also a cheap evening Artisan Class is held. Further information can be obtained by letter, addressed to the Secretary, Science and Art Department. Nearest Railway Station, South Kensington. There are also numerous Schools of Art in different parts of London associated with what is called the Kensington system, and the ROYAL ACADEMY SCHOOLS in which those are educated free who are first able to prepare the works necessary to pass the Examinations.

ART UNION OF LONDON, 112, Strand (Near the Savoy).—Has for many years issued popular Engravings, by subscription, in connection with the Annual Art Union.

ASCOT.—Celebrated for its Races held in the height of the London Season, in June, which are attended by the principal members of the Royal Family, who drive up the course in state, and by the fashionable world in general.

ATHLETICS.—The leading club is the London Athletic Club. It has a large number of members and excellent grounds at Stamford Bridge, Fulham, opposite Chelsea Station. The German Gymnastic Society, at 26, Pancras Road, King's Cross, is one of the most successful Gymnastic Clubs in London, and is composed equally of English and German members.

AVENUE THEATRE is situated at the south end of Northumberland Avenue, Charing Cross.

BALHAM.—A residential suburb about five miles from Victoria Station (L. B. & S. C. R.)

BANK OF ENGLAND (THE) THREADNEEDLE STREET.—No one visiting or travelling through the City of London by omnibus can fail to note the "Bank," a term which is reiterated by so many of the conductors of the omnibuses plying between any of the main thoroughfares. It is probable that most people coming first in sight of it will be disappointed at its somewhat stunted appearance, being one storey high. It covers, however, an area of nearly four acres. The Bank of England is the only bank in London which has the power of issuing its own notes; and it is probable that these notes are more largely distributed and more easily negotiable than those issued by any other bank in the world. The Bank transacts all business connected with the National Debt, and the dividends on Government Stock are all issued from there. It is governed by a Governor, a Deputy Governor, and a body of 24 Directors. A guard of soldiers is garrisoned at night in the Bank for the protection of the huge wealth stored there. By special privilege visitors are admitted to the different departments of the Bank, and a mill on pound note is shown them. The office hours are 9 to 4. There are branches at Burlington Gardens and adjoining the Law Courts, and in the principal cities.

BANKS.—Other large London banks are the National Provincial Bank of England; Glyn Mills & Co.; Barclay & Company (better known as Barclay, Bevan, Tritton & Co.); Robarts, Lubbock & Co.; London & Westminster; London & County Union; London City and Midland: The London Joint Stock Bank; Parr's; Lloyd's, etc.; and for small accounts notably the Birkbeck, in Holborn.

BANKERS' CLEARING HOUSE, near the Post Office, Lombard St., is where the bankers obtain the amount of cheques and bills in their hands for collection from other Banks.

BARBERS' SURGEONS' COURT ROOM, Monkwell Street, Cripplegate, is one of the few old City Halls that escaped the Great Fire ; it contains several objects of interest and some good pictures.

BARCLAY'S BREWERY stands on the site of the Globe Theatre at Bankside, Southwark, and is one of the sights of London. Visitors are occasionally admitted on written application being made.

BARKING. Near Woolwich ; Barking Creek is on the left (Essex) Bank.—Here are situated the outlets of London's new drainage system.

BARNARD'S INN. South side of Holborn, opposite Furnival's Inn ; was one of the Inns of Chancery. Is now reconstructed and used as the Mercers' Company School.

BARNES. On the right bank of the Thames between Putney and Mortlake.—A good place for a view of the Oxford and Cambridge Boat Race.

BARNET, or HIGH BARNET, about 11 miles from London : at Hadley, near, a battle was fought in 1471 between Edward IV. and the Earl of Warwick, who was defeated and slain in this last but one conflict of the Roses.

BARNSBURY adjoins Islington.

BARRACKS.—CHELSEA (Infantry).—Nearest Railway Stations, Sloane Square and Grosvenor Road.

HYDE PARK, Knightsbridge (Cavalry).—Nearest Railway Station, High Street, Kensington.

KENSINGTON, Church Street (Cavalry and Infantry).—Nearest Railway Station, High Street, Kensington.

REGENT'S PARK, Albany Street (Cavalry).—Nearest Railway Station, Portland Road.

ST. GEORGE'S, Trafalgar Square (Infantry and Recruiting).—Nearest Railway Station, Charing Cross.

ST. JOHN'S WOOD, Ordnance Road (Cavalry).—Nearest Railway Station, Marlborough Road.

TOWER (Infantry, Artillery, and Royal Engineers).—Nearest Railway Station, Tower of London (Met.).

WELLINGTON, Birdcage Walk (Infantry).—Nearest Railway Station, St. James's Park.

BATHS.—ALBANY BATHS.—83, York Road, Westminster Bridge Road.—Swimming Bath.

ARGYLL BATHS.—Warm, Vapour, and Medicated Baths, etc., 10, Argyll Place, Regent Street.

BLOOMSBURY BATHS.—Endell Street, Bloomsbury.—Baths and Public Wash-houses.

HALEY'S BATHS, 182 & 184, Euston Road.—Turkish Baths for Ladies and Gentlemen.

CHELSEA, 171, King's Road, Chelsea.—Swimming and Public Wash-house.

CROWN BATHS, Kennington Oval.—Swimming Bath.

HAMMON'S TURKISH BATHS, 76, Jermyn Street.

KENSINGTON, Lancaster Road.—Public Wash-house.

LAMBETH, 156, Westminster Bridge Road.—Swimming Bath and Public Wash-house.

NEVILL'S TURKISH BATHS, Northumberland Avenue, etc.

PADDINGTON BATHS, Queen's Road, Bayswater.—Swimming.

ST. GEORGE'S BATHS, 8, Davies Street, Berkeley Square.—Swimming and Public Wash-house.

ST. MARTIN'S, Orange Street, Leicester Square.—Public Wash-house, Hot Baths, etc.

ST. MARYLEBONE PUBLIC BATHS AND WASH-HOUSES, 181, Marylebone Road.

SAVOY, Lancaster Mansions, Savoy Street.—Turkish Baths.

WESTMINSTER BATHS, Buckingham Palace Road, S.W., and Orange Street, Leicester Square, S.W.

The above are only a few of the Baths and Wash-houses in London. There many others beside.

(*See* LONDON DIRECTORIES.)

BATTERSEA PARK. About 200 acres in extent. On the Surrey side of the River Thames in the S.W. district. One of the youngest of the London Parks ; there is every accomodation for cricketers, and boating may be indulged in on the lake. It has a very pretty sub-tropical garden which no visitor should fail to see.

BATTLE BRIDGE was situated near King's Cross ; the name was derived from a battle between the Romans and Britons in A.D. 60, in which the Romans were victorious.

BAYSWATER.—A large district containing good houses in the Parish of Paddington.

BECKENHAM.—A village in Kent, on the L. C. & D and Mid-Kent Railways.

BEDFORD SQUARE. Near Tottenham Court Road.—Lord Loughborough lived at No. 6, and in the same house Lord Chancellor Eldon lived for some years.

BELGRAVE SQUARE is situated in the fashionable region of Belgravia; the name Belgrave is derived from a village in Leicestershire where the Duke of Westminster has property.

BELGRAVIA.—A very fashionable part of London, situated between Grosvenor Place and Chelsea.

BELLE SAUVAGE, LUDGATE HILL.—An Inn on Ludgate Hill where dramas were played before regular theatres were established in England. In later years it was a great coaching inn: It is now built over by Cassell's Printing Works.

BENTLEY PRIORY, near Harrow Station (L. & N.W.R.), was used as an Hotel. Queen Adelaide died here, December 2, 1849.

BERKELEY SQUARE contains many houses of the nobility. Lansdowne House is the town house of the Marquis of Lansdowne. No. 38 is the town residence of Lord Rosebery.

BERMONDSEY adjoins the Borough of Southwark; was the seat of an ancient priory. Now celebrated for its trade and manufacture of leather, originally established by Huguenot refugees.

BETHLEHEM HOSPITAL, popularly called Bedlam, is situated in Lambeth Road, and is a large building 900 feet long with a large dome in the centre. Is a charitable institution for the insane.

BETHNAL GREEN MUSEUM is a branch of the South Kensingtom Museum. Admission free from 10 a.m to 10 p.m. on Monday, and from 10 a.m. to 4, 5 or 6 p.m. on other days. On Sundays open from 2 till dusk. Nearest Railway Station, Cambridge Heath (G.E.).

BIG BEN is the name of the great bell in the Clock Tower of the Houses of Parliament. The bell that used to be celebrated at Westminster was Great Tom, but that was removed to St. Paul's in 1699. St. Paul's has also another larger bell called Great Paul, set up in 1882 in the Dean's Tower.

BILLINGSGATE.—THE GREAT LONDON FISH MARKET; so called, according to Geoffrey of Monmouth, after Bilin, King of the Britons, who built the first water-gate here 400 years B.C. It stands on the left bank of the river, a little below London Bridge. The language of Billingsgate is not noted for its refinement. The Market is open at 5 a.m.

BIRDCAGE WALK is situated on the South side of St. James's Park. So called on account of an aviary being kept here for many years.

BISHOPSGATE.—One of the City gates, called after Erkenwald, Bishop of London. It is now removed; it stood at the corner of Camomile and Wormwood Streets.

BISLEY is now the headquarters for the Volunteers' Rifle Shooting instead of Wimbledon; it is 29 miles from Waterloo Station. Brookwood is the nearest station, distant about 2 miles from the camp; the trains run very frequently from Waterloo Station, and a branch train conveys passengers to the camp from Brookwood Station. Fares 4/6, 3/-, 2/3½; Return, 8/-, 5/2, 4/-. Sunday (return), 8/-, 4/-, 2/6.

BLACKFRIARS BRIDGE was built in 1864-9, and cost £320,000. The original Blackfriars Bridge was at first called Pitt Bridge. Close here at the wide part of Bridge Street was Chatham Place, and at No. 8, the house of Dr. Budd, a Physician at St. Bartholomew's Hospital, Lord Nelson's Lady Hamilton, when Emma Lyon, lived as nursery-maid; at the same time the housemaid at Dr. Budd's was Mrs. Powell, afterwards celebrated for her beauty and talents as an actress. A fine view of the dome of St. Paul's is to be obtained from the Thames adjacent to this bridge.

BLACKHEATH is about 7 miles from Charing Cross Station. This was the headquarters of the insurgents under Wat Tyler in 1381, and Jack Cade in 1450.

BLACKWALL.—The East India Docks are situated here, where the principal sailing ships from London load and discharge. Adjoining is the shipbuilding yard of Messrs. Green.

BLEEDING HEART YARD, mentioned in Dickens Novel of "Little Dorrit," is situated on the south side of Charles Street, Hatton Garden.

BLOOMSBURY.—A district near New Oxford Street.

BLOOMSBURY SQUARE, Near Southampton Street, High Holborn, contains a statue to Charles James Fox. The College of Preceptors is located in this square, also the Pharmaceutical Society of Great Britain (well-known to every Chemist in the country).

BLUECOAT SCHOOL, or more properly Christ's Hospital, was situated in Newgate Street, and dates from the time of Edward VI. It stood on the site of the old monastery of Grey Friars. The dress of the Bluecoat Boy is well known, consisting of a long blue gown, yellow stockings, and knee-breeches. The school is now removed to Horsham, where fine new school-buildings are erected. It is to be hoped the change of residence will not also destroy the quaint costume and the general intention of the foundation for the education and maintenance of those whose parents' income is insufficient to properly provide for them.

LONDON BRIDGE.

LONDON BRIDGE, built of granite, in five arches, from the designs of Sir John Rennie, was opened by King William IV. and Queen Adelaide in 1831. It is the great main thoroughfare between the City and the Borough of Southwark, and is the most crowded bridge in London. The Monument of the Great Fire in Fish Street Hill is near, and below the Bridge is the Wharf from which the Margate and other Excursion Steamboats start. Farther down are Billingsgate Market, the Custom House, the Tower, etc.

BOND STREET, OLD AND NEW, runs from Piccadilly to Oxford Street, and is probably the most fashionable shopping street of the West End.

BOROUGH (THE) is on the Surrey side of London Bridge. A very busy part of London. Head-quarters of the hop trade.

BOTANIC SOCIETY (ROYAL) OF LONDON.—The Gardens of the Society, nearly twenty acres in extent, comprise the whole of the Inner Circle of Regent's Park. Admission by Member's Tickets.

BOW BELLS. In Bow Church, Cheapside.—It is said that all those persons who are born within the sound of Bow Bells are Cockneys.

BOX HILL. Near Dorking.—Celebrated for its beautiful scenery; about 30 miles from London on the South Eastern or Brighton Railway.

BREAD STREET. CHEAPSIDE—on south side.—So called from bread being sold here in old times. Milton was born in this street in 1608.

BRENTFORD.—An old town about 7 miles from London, on the Middlesex side of the Thames. Canute was defeated by Edmund Ironside here in 1016.

BRENTWOOD. ESSEX.—About 18 miles from London by rail from Liverpool Street.

BRICKLAYERS' ARMS. OLD KENT ROAD.—A celebrated tavern and coach-house, at the corner of Bermondsey New Road and Old Kent Road, lately rebuilt; but the name dates back more than 500 years. It has given its name to the large goods station of the South Eastern Railway.

BRIGHTON.—"London by the Sea," as it is called.—A favourite seaside place in Sussex, distant about 50 miles from London, has a magnificent sea front, and, in addition to the many Londoners who now make it their residence, is a popular visiting place for those who have to live in town. The fashionable season is in the late autumn. The London, Brighton and South Coast Railway through trains from London Bridge or Victoria do the journey in a little over an hour, and there are frequent cheap day excursions.

BRITANNIA THEATRE. HOXTON.—A very well constructed theatre in a crowded thoroughfare. Nearest Railway Station, Shoreditch (N. L.).

BRITISH MUSEUM (THE). GREAT RUSSELL STREET, BLOOMSBURY.—A huge building in the classic style of architecture, completed in 1845, for the exhibition of antiquities:—Marbles, Manuscripts, Bas-reliefs, Greek and Roman Sculptures, Vases, Bronzes, Gold Ornaments and Gems, etc., etc. The Great Reading Room (permission to regularly use which is to be obtained from the principal Librarian) was built in 1857, and is a huge circular structure with a dome. Visitors to the Museum are allowed to look into this room from the doorway. The Libraries of the Museum comprise 2,000,000 volumes, and as a copy of each book published is required to be deposited there the increase annually is very considerable. Open to the public daily:—On weekdays from 10 a.m. to 6 p.m. After 4 p.m. in January, February, November, December, and after 5 p.m. in March, September, October, only certain of the galleries remain open, viz :—On Mondays, Wednesdays and Fridays, Exhibitions of Manuscripts, Printed Books, Prints and Drawings, Porcelain, Glass, and Majolica; Prehistoric, British, Anglo-Saxon, Mediæval and Ethnographical Collections. On Tuesdays, Thursdays and Saturdays, Egyptian, Assyrian, Greek and Roman Galleries (exclusive of the Vase Rooms and Bronze Room), American Collections, and the Waddesdon Room. On Sunday afternoons:—From 2 to 4 p.m. in January, February, November, December; from 2 to 5 p.m. in October; from 2 to 5.30 p.m. in March, September; from 2 to 6 p.m. April, May, June, July, August. The Museum is closed on Good Friday and on Christmas Day. Guide-books are sold in the Museum.

BRITISH MUSEUM OF NATURAL HISTORY.—The Departments of Zoology, Geology, Mineralogy, and Botany have been removed from Great Russell Street to Cromwell Road, South Kensington. Open daily, free, at 10 a.m.; January, till 4 p.m.; February, 4.30 p.m.; March, 5.30 p.m.; April to August, 6 p.m.; October, 5 p.m.; November and December, ± p.m. Open Sundays 2 to 4 p.m. January, November and December; February, 4.30 p.m.; March, 5.30 p.m.; May to August, 2.30 to 7 p.m.

BRIXTON.—A southern suburb of London, adjoining Clapham, easily reached by omnibus or rail.

BROAD SANCTUARY is where the Westminster Hospital now stands, and is the site of the ancient Sanctuary of Westminster; in old times, any debtor or criminal who could get within the bounds of Sanctuary was for the time protected from arrest. Near here was set up the first printing press ever used in England, by William Caxton, in the year 1474.

BROAD STREET STATION, N. L. and L. & N. W., is adjacent to the G. E. R., Liverpool Street terminus, and Met. R., Bishopsgate Street. This neighbourhood, through the large railway traffic (suburban and East Coast), is one of the busiest in the City.

BROMLEY, IN MIDDLESEX, is a few miles from Fenchurch Street Station.

BROMLEY IN KENT, is pleasantly situated about 12 miles from Charing Cross Station.

BROOKE STREET, HOLBORN.—In this street the poet Chatterton put an end to his life with arsenic, on August 24, 1779, at the age of 17 years and 9 months. It has been mostly rebuilt, and at the end of it is the well-known church of St. Alban's, Holborn. A memorial chapel to Mr. Mackonochie is added to it. The services of this church are noted for their full ritualistic character. A very handsome triptych has recently been placed over the altar. Adjoining this street in Holborn are the huge palatial buildings of the Prudential Insurance Company.

BROXBOURNE.—A holiday resort on the Great Eastern Railway. Near here is Rye House, the scene of the Rye House plot, a scheme to assassinate Charles II.

BUCKINGHAM PALACE is at the west end of St. James's Park, and was built in 1825 by the order of George IV. The King and Queen reside here now that it has been prepared for their reception. The Royal Mews may be viewed by applying to the Master of the Horse for an order. The stables, the coach-houses, and the grand State Carriage, designed in 1762 for George III., used for the opening of Parliament by King Edward VII. and also for the Coronation Procession, are worth seeing. It has been decided that the great national memorial to Queen Victoria shall be erected in front of the Palace, with an avenue through the Mall to Charing Cross.

BUNHILL FIELDS.—A celebrated burial place of the Nonconformists. Open daily from 9 till 4, and on Sunday after 1 o'clock. John Bunyan, the author of " Pilgrim's Progress," was buried here; Isaac Watts, author of so many hymns: and Daniel Defoe, author of "Robinson Crusoe," and other famous men are buried here ; John Wesley was buried near here, in a chapel in City Road.

BURLINGTON ARCADE. PICCADILLY.—A double row of fashionable shops like a Parisian passage. Nearest Railway Station, St. James's Park (Dis.).

BURLINGTON HOUSE. PICCADILLY.—The home of the Royal Academy of Arts University of London, and other Societies.

BURNHAM BEECHES, near Slough, purchased by the Corporation of London, are said to be the finest in England, and can be reached by G. W. R. Motor Service from Slough.

BUSHEY PARK leads from the Teddington Road to Hampton Court Palace, and has a fine avenue of chestnut trees. In May, when these trees are in full bloom, "Chestnut Sunday" brings an enormous crowd of visitors to enjoy the beautiful sight. Rail from Waterloo to Teddington, thence through the park to the palace.

CAMBERWELL. SURREY.—A large parish ; it includes Peckham and Dulwich.

CAMDEN TOWN is in the Parish of ST. PANCRAS, between Somers Town and Kentish Town. The "Mother Red Cap" Inn, at the end of High Street, was for many years the stopping place of omnibuses.

CANNING TOWN.—A river-side district on Plaistow Level to the east of the Lea river, near its mouth ; the Victoria Docks are situated here.

CANONBURY, a manor in Islington, given in old times to the Priory of St. Bartholomew, Smithfield. Canonbury Tower, a relic of this Priory, still stands in Canonbury Square.

CANVEY ISLAND, ESSEX.—On the Thames, about 12 miles below Gravesend, near Thames Haven. Reclaimed from the estuary by some Dutch settlers in time of Charles II.

CAPEL COURT, BARTHOLOMEW LANE.—So called from Sir William Capel, draper, Lord Mayor of London in 1503, the ancestor of the Earls of Essex. The Stock Exchange is situated here.

CATHEDRAL RAILWAY ROUTE (THE) from Liverpool to London is so called because, at the same fares charged by the direct routes, passengers are enabled to visit the Cathedrals of Manchester, Lincoln, Ely, and the University of Cambridge, and, at small additional expense, Peterborough and Norwich. This route is of great interest to Americans travelling from Liverpool to London or the Continent *via* Harwich.

CAVENDISH SQUARE adjoins HARLEY STREET.—Contains an equestrian statue to William, Duke of Cumberland, the hero of Culloden; also a statue to Lord George Bentinck. This Square used to be very fashionable. The whole neighbourhood is now largely tenanted by the leading physicians, surgeons, and dentists.

CEMETERIES.—The following are the principal London Cemeteries:

ABNEY PARK.—Office, Stoke Newington, N. Nearest Railway Station, Stoke Newington (G.E.). From Liverpool Street, 18 min.

CAMBERWELL.—Nearest Railway Station, Honor Oak (L.C. & D.). From Ludgate Hill, 27 min.

CITY OF LONDON, Manor Park.—**From** Liverpool Street, 25 min.

GREAT NORTHERN.—Office, 22, Great Winchester Street, E.C. Nearest Railway Station, New Southgate (G.N.). From King's Cross, 50 min.

HAMPSTEAD.—Nearest Railway Station, Child's Hill (Midland). From St. Pancras, 23 min.

HANWELL.—Nearest Railway Station, Hanwell (G.W.) From Paddington, 25 min.

HIGHGATE.—Office, 22, New Bridge Street, E.C. Nearest Railway Station, Upper Holloway and Highgate Road (Tottenham and Hampstead Junction). From St. Pancras, 12 min.

JEWS' BURIAL GROUND, Mile End Road, N.—Nearest Railway Station, Whitechapel (E.L.). From Liverpool Street, 4 min. 1st, -/4, -/6 ; 2nd, -/3, -/5: 3rd, -/2, -/4. Old Ford (G.E.). From Liverpool Street, 10 min. 1st, -/6, -/9 ; 2nd, -/4, -/6 ; 3rd, -/3, -/5. Bethnal Green Junction (G.E.). From Liverpool Street, 5 min.

KENSAL GREEN.—Office, 95, Great Russell Street, W.C. Nearest Railway Station, Kensal Green (L. & N.W.). From Broad Street, 33 min.

NORWOOD.—Nearest Railway Station, Lower Norwood (L.B. & S.C.). From London Bridge, 34 min.

NUNHEAD, Peckham Rye.—Office, 29, New Bridge Street, E.C. Nearest Railway Station, Nunhead (L.C. & D.). From Ludgate Hill, 26 min.

PADDINGTON.—Nearest Railway Stations, Kilburn (L. & N.W.). From Broad Street, 45 min. 1st, -/9, 1/-: 2nd, -/6, -/9. Edgware Road (Met.). From Aldgate, 24 min.

ST. MARYLEBONE, East End, Finchley.—Office, Town Hall, Marylebone Lane. Nearest Railway Station, East Finchley. From King's Cross, 21 min.

WEST OF LONDON AND WESTMINSTER.—Office, 12, Haymarket, S.W. Nearest Railway Station, West Brompton, 19 min. Chelsea, 15 min. From Mansion House, 23 min.

WOKING.—Offices, 2, Lancaster Place, W.C., and Westminster Bridge Road, S.E. Nearest Railway Station, Brookwood (S.W.). From Waterloo, about 1 hour.

The times for visiting the Cemeteries vary with the seasons of the year. On Sundays in the afternoons only, and they are generally closed on Bank Holidays.

CENTRAL LONDON RAILWAY (THE), familiarly known to Londoners as the "Tube," is an underground Electric Railway from the Bank to Shepherd's Bush, *via* Holborn, Oxford Street, Bond Street, Hyde Park, and Notting Hill. It is a very speedy and convenient method of communication between the City and West London. The fare is 2d. any distance.

CHALK FARM, near PRIMROSE HILL, SOUTH HAMPSTEAD.—Chalk Farm was a white-washed Public-house, known, in 1678, as the "White House," with a Tea Garden, and was the scene of many duels.

CHANCERY LANE extends from Fleet Street to Holborn, and is considered the principal legal thoroughfare in London. The Record Office is now extended, and has a fine frontage in Chancery Lane.

CHARING CROSS derives its name from the little village of Cherringe, which was situated half-way between London and Westminster. About 1291 Edward I. erected a cross here in memory of his wife, Queen Eleanor, whose body was brought from Nottinghamshire to Westminster Abbey. Each of the nine resting places was similarly marked. The original Cross stood from 1291 until 1647. The modern reproduction is by Mr. Durham, R.A. Cab fares are computed from Charing Cross, which has been described as the "legal centre of London."

CHARTER HOUSE in CHARTERHOUSE SQUARE, near Aldersgate Street, was originally founded in 1371: the chapel, which contains the superb tomb of the founder, is worth seeing. The Merchant Taylors' School adjoins.

CHATHAM, on the East bank of the Medway below Rochester.—**One of** the chief Naval Arsenals and Military Stations.

CHEAPSIDE. Extends from Newgate Street to the Poultry.—The names of the streets leading from Cheapside are mostly named after what was sold in them in olden times, such as Wood, Milk, Bread, Honey, Poultry, &c. (Bread Street was the birthplace of John Milton.) All these streets constitute, with part of Cannon Street and St. Paul's Churchyard, the centre of the Wholesale Drapery Trade in London. Morleys' Cooks', Dents', &c., are household words amongst drapers all over the country.

CHEAPSIDE.—One of the most crowded thoroughfares in London—runs from Newgate Street and St. Paul's Churchyard to the Bank, Mansion House and Royal Exchange.

BOW CHURCH is memorable for the bells which Dick Whittington heard on Highgate Hill, calling him back to be Lord Mayor of London. It is said that all those born within sound of Bow Bells are cockneys.—*From a Photograph by the London Stereoscopic Company,* 54, *Cheapside.*

CHELSEA. On the left bank of the Thames, three miles from London.—Here, at 24, formerly 5, Cheyne Row, lived Thomas Carlyle ; he died here on February 5th, 1881, and his house is now fitted up as a memorial museum, open from 10 a.m. till sunset, admission 1s. The rare old Chelsea china was made here at the waterside.

CHELSEA EMBANKMENT extends from Chelsea Hospital to Battersea Bridge, about ⅔ of a mile ; was opened on May 9th, 1874.

CHELSEA HOSPITAL.—One of the most interesting sights of London. Was built by Charles II. The foundation stone was laid in 1682 by the King himself. It is generally supposed that it was Nell Gwynne's influence with the King which caused him to establish this splendid hospital for old soldiers. In the Dining Hall and Chapel are battle flags taken by the British Army in all parts of the world. The gardens are open to the public and the Sunday services at the Chapel also open to visitors.

CHERTSEY, SURREY.—On right bank of Thames from Oxford ; about 20 miles from London by river ; an old-fashioned, quiet town. Virginia water is near here.

CHESHUNT.—14 miles from Liverpool Street Station ; has a College for the education of young men for the Noncomformist ministry.

CHIGWELL.—13 miles from Liverpool Street Station ; alluded to in some of Charles Dickens's novels, especially " Barnaby Rudge."

CHINGFORD. Adjoining EPPING FOREST.—The Royal Forest Hotel here is much used by visitors to the Forest.

CHISLEHURST. In Kent.—Napoleon III. resided here at Camden Place, and, dying on January 9th, 1873, was buried in the little church near ; but his remains, and those of his son, the Prince Imperial, have now been removed to Farnborough, Hampshire.

CHISWICK. 5 miles from London.—In Chiswick Churchyard, are buried William Hogarth, and Mary, third daughter of Oliver Cromwell.

CHRIST'S HOSPITAL, for many years in Newgate Street, is now removed to Horsham.—Presentations to this School, which maintains, and educates about 1,100 children can be obtained from the Governors under certain regulations. (*See* BLUECOAT SCHOOL.)

CHURCHES AND CHAPELS.—The following are some of the best known places of worship. As there are about 1,300 Churches and Chapels in greater London, these are given as being most convenient for the ordinary Visitor.

CHURCH OF ENGLAND.

	DAILY SERVICES.	SUNDAY SERVICES. Morning. Afternoon. Evening.
WESTMINSTER ABBEY	10 a.m. 3 p.m.	8 a.m. 10 a.m. 3 p.m. At certain Seasons, services in the Nave, 7 p.m.
ST. PAUL'S CATHEDRAL	10 a.m. 4 p.m.	8 a.m. 10.30 a.m. 3.15 p.m. 7 p.m.

See page |

ST. SAVIOUR'S COLLEGIATE CHURCH, SOUTHWARK.—Twelfth century building, recently restored and new nave added. Probably the future cathedral for South London. *Sunday Services*, 11 a.m. and 7 p.m.

SAVOY CHAPEL, in a turning out of the Strand. *Sunday Services*, 11 a.m. and 7 p.m.

THE TEMPLE CHURCH, The Inner Temple, Fleet Street.—One of the oldest churches in London. The Round Church was built in 1185, and the Gothic choir in 1240. The music at the Temple services is always well rendered. Admission on Sundays by Bencher's order. *Sunday Services*, 11 a.m. and 3 p.m.

ST. BARTHOLMEW'S THE GREAT, West Smithfield.—An older church still than the Temple; date 1123. Is a Norman building which escaped the Great Fire of London in 1666, which was stopped at Pye Corner, close to St. Batholomew's Hospital. *Sunday Services*, 11 a.m., 4 p.m., and 7 p.m.

BOW CHURCH, Cheapside, by Sir Christopher Wren, has a fine tower, and is well known for its peal of bells, which were supposed to have recalled Dick Whittington back from Highgate to be "Lord Mayor of London Town." *Sunday Services*, 11 a.m and 7 p.m.

ST. MICHAEL'S, Cornhill, and ST. PETER'S, Cornhill, ST. EDMUND KING AND MARTYR, Lombard Street. *Sunday Services*, 11 a.m. and 7 p.m.

ST. NICHOLAS COLE ABBEY, Queen Victoria Street. *Sunday Services*, 10.30 a.m. and 7 p.m.

ST. BRIDE's Fleet Street. *Sunday Services*, 11 a.m. and 7 p.m.

ST. CLEMENT'S DANES, Strand.—Where Dr. Johnson used to attend. One of the two churches destined to remain in the centre of this well known and widened thoroughfare. *Sunday Services*, 11 a.m. and 7 p.m.

ST. MARY-LE-STRAND.—*Sunday Services*, 11 a.m. 7 p.m.

ST. ALBAN'S, Brooke Street, Holborn.—Well known for its ritualistic services. *Sunday Services*, 11 a.m., 3.15 p.m., and 7 p.m.

FOUNDLING CHAPEL, Guildford Street, Gray's Inn Road.—Is the place of worship attached to the Foundling Hospital, which is open to the public every Sunday on payment of a small offering at the doors, and is one of the most interesting places of worship in London. The music has long been a special attraction, and the choir, which is composed of the children themselves, is assisted by distinguished singers. A very handsome suite of rooms, containing some valuable pictures, curiosities, &c., can also be seen after service at 11 a.m. Nearest Railway Stations, King's Cross and St. Pancras. *Sunday Services*, 11 a.m. and 3.30 p.m.

ST. MARTIN'S-IN-THE-FIELDS, Trafalgar Square.—*Sunday Services*, 11 a.m. and 7 p.m.

In the WEST END—ALL SAINTS', Margaret Street; ST. ANDREW'S, Well Street; ST. PETER'S, Eaton Square; are well known for their musical services. Whilst ST. MICHAEL'S, Chester Square (Can n Fleming), and ST. JAMES's, Westmoreland Place, are also representative churches. *Sunday Services*, 11 a.m. and 7 p.m.

WESLEYANS.
CITY ROAD CHAPEL.

GREAT QUEEN STREET CHAPEL, Lincoln's-Inn-Fields. *Sunday Services*, 11 a.m. and 6.30 p.m.

CONGREGATIONALISTS.
CITY TEMPLE, Holborn Viaduct (Rev. R. J. Campbell).—*Sunday Services*, 11 a.m. and 7 p.m.

CHRIST CHURCH, Westminster Bridge Road. *Sunday Services*, 11 a.m. and 7 p.m.

BAPTIST.

METROPOLITAN TABERNACLE (Mr. Spurgeon's), Newington Butts.—*Sunday Services* 11 *a.m.* and 6.30 *p.m.*

WESTBOURNE PARK CHAPEL (Dr. Clifford), *Sunday Services*, 11 *a.m.* and 7 *p.m.*

PARK SQUARE CHAPEL, Regent's Park.—*Sunday Services*, 11 *a.m.* and 7 *p.m.*

PRESBYTERIANS.

SCOTTISH NATIONAL CHURCH, Pont Street, Belgravia.—*Sunday Services*, 11 *a.m.* and 7 *p.m.*

REGENT'S SQUARE CHURCH, Gray's Inn Road—*Sunday Services*, 11 *a.m.* and 7 *p.m.*

WELSH CALVANISTIC METHODIST CHAPEL (NEW JEWIN). FANN STREET, ALDERS-GATE STREET. *Sunday Services*, 10.45 *a m.* and 6.30 *p.m.*

ROMAN CATHOLICS.

ST. GEORGE'S CATHEDRAL, Southwark.—*Sunday Services*, 11 *a.m.* and 7 *p.m.*

PRO-CATHEDRAL, High Street, Kensington.—*Sunday Services*, 11 *a.m.* and 7 *p.m.*

THE BROMPTON ORATORY, South Kensington.—*Sunday Services*, 11 *a.m* and 7 *p.m.*

ROMAN CATHOLIC CATHEDRAL, Ashley Place, Westminster.

CATHOLIC APOSTOLIC CHURCH, Gordon Square, near Euston Road.—*Sunday Services*, 10 *a.m.*, 2 *p.m.*, and 5 *p.m.*

CITY OF LONDON.—The E.C. District of London practically comprises the City, and is under the rule of the Corporation of London, headed by the Lord Mayor, whose official residence is the Mansion House. The Lord Mayor's Show is one of the sights of London on Nov. 9th, and, although threatened as an institution, still seems to live.

CITY COMPANIES.—The twelve great City Companies in order of civic precedence are the Mercers, Grocers, Drapers, Fishmongers, Goldsmiths, Skinners, Merchant Taylors, Haberdashers, Salters, Ironmongers, Vintners and Clothworkers.—There are about 80 companies, but only about half have halls of their own. Originally they were trades guilds regulating and controlling their own particular business, but most of them have long ceased to represent their trades except in name.

CITY OF LONDON SCHOOL, is situated on the Thames Embankment near Blackfriars Bridge. Established by the City Corporation in 1834, and is one of the large and very successful public middle-class day schools of the Metropolis.

CLAPHAM COMMON is situated on the Surrey side of the Thames: in extent it is about 220 acres, and is suitable for cricket, etc. Lord Macaulay, when a boy, used to attend the old church on Clapham Common.

CLARE MARKET is situated on the western side of Lincoln's Inn Fields. It is a collection of small shops, stalls, etc. Near here was the site of the ancient palace of John, Earl of Clare, who resided here about 1617, hence the name Clare Market. The new road from the Strand to Holborn will clear this neighbourhood.

CLEMENT'S INN, STRAND, one of the Inns of Chancery, near St. Clement's Church.

CLEOPATRA'S NEEDLE. On the Victoria Embankment. This famous monument of granite from Alexandria originally stood at Heliopolis, and was presented to this country by Mehemet Ali, in 1819. It is 68 feet high, and weighs 180 tons. Nearest Railway Station, Charing Cross.

CLERKENWELL.—A parish extending northwards from Holborn. It was originally a village around the Priory of St. John of Jerusalem, of which the gate-house still remains. Isaak Walton lived here in 1650.

CLIFFORD'S INN.—One of the old Inns of Chancery, near St. Dunstan's Church, Fleet Street.

COACHING CLUBS.—Many pleasant daily excursions may be made on the well-appointed coaches that run out of London. The following are some of the favourite drives: Windsor, Dorking, St. Albans, Guildford, Virginia Water, etc., etc. See Excursions by Coach.

COAL EXCHANGE, LOWER THAMES STREET, near the Custom House. Opened in 1849.

COCKNEY.—This is a term commonly applied to those persons who are born within the sound of the bells of Bow Church, in Cheapside.

ST. PAUL'S CATHEDRAL, the most conspicuous building in London. Tradition says that it stands on the site of the original building erected in the second century. St. Paul's was entirely destroyed in the Great Fire of London, and was rebuilt about 1673 **by Sir** Christopher Wren. Lord Nelson and the Duke of Wellington are buried here.—*From a Photograph by Bedford, Lemere & Co,*

COLLEGE OF SURGEONS (ROYAL). LINCOLN'S INN FIELDS.—**Very interesting** to professional visitors. Nearest Railway Station, Temple (District).

COLNEY HATCH, 7 miles from London.—There is a large Lunatic Asylum here. Station, New Southgate.

COLONIAL OFFICE, WHITEHALL.—Where the official business between Great Britain and her Colonies is conducted.

COLUMBIA MARKET, BETHNAL GREEN, was erected by the Baroness Burdett-Coutts for the benefit of the East End people.

COMEDY THEATRE, PANTON STREET, Haymarket, W.

COMMISSIONAIRES' OFFICE, 419a, STRAND.—Parcels or Messages are carried at the rate of 3d. per mile or 6d. per hour; extra for parcels over 14 lbs.

CONSTITUTION HILL is situated in the Green Park, along the wall of Buckingham Palace Gardens.

COLONIAL AGENTS:
> BRITISH COLUMBIA, Office, 15, Serjeant's Inn, Temple, E.C.
> CANADA. Office, 17, Victoria Street, S.W.
> CAPE COLONY, Office, 98 & 100, Victoria Street, S.W.
> NATAL, Office, 26, Victoria Street, S.W.
> NEW SOUTH WALES, Office, Westminster Chambers, 9, Victoria Street, S.W.
> NEW ZEALAND, Westminster Chambers, 13, Victoria Street, S.W.
> QUEENSLAND, Office, 1, Victoria Street, S.W.
> SOUTH AUSTRALIA, 1, Crosby Square, E.C.
> TASMANIA, Office, Westminster Chambers, 5, Victoria Street, S.W.
> VICTORIA, Office, 15, Victoria Street, S.W.
> WESTERN AUSTRALIA, 15, Victoria Street, S.W.

COOKHAM, BERKSHIRE, on the right bank of the River Thames, about 53 miles from London by the river.—Cookham stands at the end of what is popularly supposed to be the best part of the Thames and, together with Maidenhead, is probably better known to London excursionists than almost any other place on the river. Railway Station, Taplow, G.W.R.

CO-OPERATIVE STORES.—The principal ones in London are: Civil Service Supply Association, 136, Queen Victoria Street, E.C.; Civil Service Co-operative Society, 28, Haymarket; Army & Navy Co-operative Society, 105, Victoria Street, S.W.; Junior Army and Navy, York House, Regent Street; New Civil Service Co-operative, 122, Queen Victoria Street, E.C.

COOPER'S HILL adjoins EGHAM, Surrey.—Cooper's Hill College is situated here, and is established for the education of Civil Engineers for the service of Government, etc.

COPENHAGEN FIELDS. Between CAMDEN TOWN and ISLINGTON.—The Metropolitan Cattle Market is held here.

CORNHILL extends from the Mansion House to Leadenhall Street. Largely occupied by Banks, Financial Companies, etc.

"**CORNWALL**" REFORMATORY TRAINING SHIP is anchored in the Thames off Purfleet.—The "Cornwall" was once the "Wellesley," and was built in Bombay of teak, in 1815.

COUNTY COUNCIL OF LONDON. Office, SPRING GARDENS, S.W.—Held its first meeting, March 21, 1889, when it took over the work of the Metropolitan Board of Works, besides other responsibilities. Has the supervision of the Parks and Open Spaces of the Metropolis.

COURT THEATRE. SLOANE SQUARE.—Light comedies and farces.

CONSULATE OFFICES:

AMERICA (United States of), 12, St. Helen's Place, Bishopgate Street, E.C.: Office of Legation, 123, Victoria Street, S.W.

ARGENTINE REPUBLIC (LA PLATA), 3, Budge Row, Cannon Street, E.C.

AUSTRIA AND HUNGARY, Office, 22 and 23, Lawrence Pountney Lane; Legation, 18, Belgrave Square, S.W.

BELGIUM, Office, 29, Great St. Helen's, E.C.; Legation, 18, Harrington Gardens, South Kensington.

BOLIVIA, Office, 12, Fenchurch Street, E.C.

BRAZIL (United States of), Office, 6, Great Winchester Street, E.C.; Legation, 11, Southwell Gardens, S.W.

CENTRAL AMERICAN REPUBLIC (including Honduras, Nicaragua, and Salvador), 7 and 8, Idol Lane, E.C.; Legation, 1, York Street, Portman Square, W.

CHILI (Republic of), 10, Lime Street, E.C.; Legation, 50, Queen's Gate Terrace, South Kensington, S.W.

CHINA, Legation, 49, Portland Place, W.

COLOMBIA (Republic of), Office, 103, Newgate Street, E.C.

COSTA RICA, Office, 58, Lombard Street, E.C.

DENMARK, Office, Muscovy Court, Tower Hill, E.C.; Legation, 24, Pont Street, S.W.

ECUADOR (Republic of), Office, 46, Lombard Street, E.C.

FRANCE, Office, 4, Christopher Street, Finsbury; Legation, Albert Gate House, Hyde Park, W.

GERMAN EMPIRE, Office, 49, Finsbury Square, E.C.; Legation, 9, Carlton House Terrace, S.W.

GREECE, Office, 19, Eastcheap, E.C.; Legation, 31, Marloes Road, S.W.

GUATEMALA (Republic of), Office, 31, Westminster Palace Gardens.

HAITI, Office, 32, Fenchurch Street, E.C.; Legation, 5, Albany Court Yard, Piccadilly, W.

ITALY, Office, 44, Finsbury Square, E.C.; Legation, 20, Grosvenor Square, W.

JAPAN, Office, 84, Bishopsgate Street, E.C.; Legation, 4, Grosvenor Gardens, S.W.

LIBERIA (Republic of), Office, 3, Coleman Street, E.C.

MEXICO, Office, Broad Street House, New Broad Street, E.C.

MONACO, Office, 37, Conduit Street, W.

NETHERLANDS, Office, 4, Coleman Street; Legation, 8, Grosvenor Gardens, S.W.

PARAGUAY (Republic of), 18, Eldon Street, E.C.

PERSIA, Legation, 120 and 122, Victoria Street, S.W.

PERU (Republic of), 104, Victoria Street. S.W.; Legation, 3, Park Place, St. James's, W.

PORTUGAL, Office, 6, South Street, Finsbury, E.C.; Legation, 12, Gloucester Place, Portman Square, W.

ROUMANIA, Office, 68, Basinghall Street, E.C.; Legation, 102, Victoria Street, S.W.

RUSSIA, Office, 17, Great Winchester Street, E.C.; Legation, Chesham House, Chesham Place, S.W.

SAN DOMINGO, Office, 17, Coleman Street, E.C.

SERVIA, Office, 9, Southampton Street, Bloomsbury, W.C.

SIAM, Office, 5 and 6, Great Winchester Street, E.C.; Legation, 23, Ashburnham Place, South Kensington, S.W.

SPAIN, Office, 20, Mark Lane, E.C.; Legation, 1, Grosvenor Gardens, S.W.

SWEDEN AND NORWAY, Office, 24, Great Winchester Street, E.C.; Legation, 52, Pont Street, S.W.

SWITZERLAND, Legation, 52, Lexham Gardens, W.

TURKEY, Office, 29, Mincing Lane, E.C.; Legation, 1, Bryanston Square, W.

URUGUAY (Republic of) (Monte Video), Office, 1A, Edinburgh Mansions, Victoria Street, S.W.

VENEZUELA (United States of), Office, Moorgate Street Chambers, E.C.

COVENT GARDEN MARKET.—Worth paying a visit to see the fruit, flowers, vegetables, etc., early in the morning from 6 to 9. Nearest Railway Station, Charing Cross.

COVENT GARDEN THEATRE.—One of the largest Theatres in London. Is principally used for Italian and English Opera.

CRICKET.—"Lord's" and the "Oval" are the principal Cricket Grounds in London. "Lord's" Cricket Ground is near St. John's Wood Road Station. The "Oval" is situated near Kennington Park. There are many other good cricket clubs and grounds in and around London.

CRIPPLEGATE WARD.—One of the 26 Wards of London. Named after one of the northern City gates of same name.

CRITERION THEATRE, REGENT CIRCUS, PICCADILLY.—This theatre is built entirely underground, but is handsome and commodious. Long associated with the name of Sir Charles Wyndham. Nearest Railway Station, Charing Cross.

CROSBY HALL, BISHOPSGATE STREET, E.C.—A fine old building of the fifteenth century; it is now used as a restaurant by Messrs. Gordon.

CROYDON.—A municipal Borough 10 miles from London, with a population of over 100,000.

CRYSTAL PALACE (THE), SYDENHAM.—About 7 miles from London. The large building was used for the Great Exhibition of 1851 in Hyde Park. The Palace is reached by frequent trains from London Bridge, Victoria, Holborn, and Ludgate Hill. Concerts, Dramatic Entertainments, Flower Shows, Cricket and other Matches, and a variety of Exhibitions are held here during the year. Brock's Fireworks are a feature of the Summer Season (especially on Thursday evenings). The Palace and Grounds cover about 200 acres. Return fares on ordinary days from 1s. third class: including admission, 1s. 9d.

CURZON STREET is situated in Mayfair, a fashionable quarter, named from a fair being held there by grant of James II.; used to commence on May 1st and last for fifteen days; was suppressed in 1708. The late Lord Beaconsfield died at his town house in this street (No. 19) on April 19th, 1881.

CUSTOM HOUSE. LOWER THAMES STREET.—Nearest Railway Station, Monument (or Mark Lane), Dis. & Met. Built 1814-17, with river facade added in 1852.

DAGENHAM. In Essex.—A village near Rainham, on London, Tilbury, and Southend line.

DALSTON.—Adjoins Kingsland Road, Hackney.

DATCHET is a village about a mile from Windsor.

DEAN'S COURT.—A turning out of St. Paul's Churchyard on the right-hand side of the western front of the Cathedral. Marriage licences are granted here.

DEAN'S YARD. Adjoins Westminster Abbey. The Church House is on the South side.

DEPTFORD. On the south bank of the Thames, opposite Limehouse.—Once a Government dockyard; now used by the Corporation of London as a market for foreign cattle.

DERBY (THE).—This race is run on Epsom Downs each year about the last week in May.

DEVONSHIRE HOUSE. PICCADILLY.—The town residence of the Duke of Devonshire. Has a gloomy frontage in one of London's finest thoroughfares.

DOCKS. London has most extensive dock accommodation.
> ST. KATHERINE'S DOCKS. Near the Tower. Nearest Railway Station, Leman Street.
> LONDON DOCKS. Near Wapping and Shadwell. Contain extensive wine vaults, also warehouses for tobacco. Nearest Railway Station, Leman Street.
> REGENT'S CANAL DOCKS, or LIMEHOUSE BASIN. At Limehouse.
> SURREY COMMERCIAL DOCKS. At Rotherhithe, near Thames Tunnel. Nearest Railway Station, Rotherhithe.
> WEST INDIA DOCKS. At Poplar. Nearest Railway Station, West India Docks.
> SOUTH WEST INDIA DOCKS. Poplar.
> MILLWALL DOCKS. At Isle of Dogs. Nearest Railway Station, Millwall.
> EAST INDIA DOCKS. At Blackwall.
> VICTORIA AND ALBERT DOCKS. Beckton, near North Woolwich. Nearest Railway Station for Victoria Docks, Tidal Basin and Custom House (G.E.).
> TILBURY DOCKS. At Tilbury. New docks opened in 1886; very extensive, and there is more water on the sill of these docks at low water than any other dock in the world.

DOCTORS' COMMONS. Near St. Paul's Churchyard.—Was a college for the study and practice of Civil Law. The Will Office used to be here, but is removed to Somerset House.

DOGGETT'S COAT AND BADGE.—Boat race rowed against the stream annually on August 1 by young watermen, from Old Swan Pier, London Bridge, to Chelsea, five miles. Founded in 1716 by Doggett, an old Drury Lane comedian.

DOMESDAY BOOK, or Survey of England, made by William the Conqueror, is preserved in the Public Record Office, near Chancery Lane.

DORKING.—A town in Surrey, situated in the midst of lovely scenery, and well worth a visit. It is about 25 miles south-west of London, and can be reached by rail or coach.

DOULTON'S CELEBRATED POTTERY (known as "Doulton Ware").—The manufactory is situated on south bank of the Thames, opposite the Tate Gallery. Attached are Schools of China Painting and Design.

DOWGATE. One of the 26 Wards of London; so called from the dock or water-gate of that name.

DOWNING STREET. WHITEHALL.—In which are the official residences of the First Lord of the Treasury and the Chancellor of the Exchequer, also the **Foreign Office, etc.** The Cabinet Councils of the Government are generally held here.

DRAPERS' HALL. In THROGMORTON STREET.—Belongs to the Drapers' Company. Contains a valuable collection of oil paintings.

DRURY LANE THEATRE, CATHERINE STREET, STRAND.—The oldest and largest Theatre in London, the home of Pantomime and Spectacular Dramas. Nearest Railway Station, Temple.

DUDLEY PICTURE GALLERY, EGYPTIAN HALL, PICCADILLY.—The pictures of the English Art Club are exhibited here in the spring.

DUKE OF YORK'S COLUMN. Near Spring Gardens, St. James's Park.—Was erected in 1833; 124 feet high. Admission 6d. between 10 and 4, from May to September.

DULWICH COLLEGE AND PICTURE GALLERY. The College was founded in 1619, by Edward Alleyn, under Letters Patent of King James I., and is now a fine School Building. Erected in 1870. One of the large middle-class schools of London. The Picture Gallery contains some fine pictures by Murillo, Poussin, and especially of Cuyp, Wouverman, Rembrandt, and others of the Dutch and Flemish Schools. Admission Free, from 10 to 4, Saturdays included, between May and September. Distance by Rail, 5 miles, London, Chatham and Dover Railway.

DYER'S HALL, 10, DOWGATE HILL. Belongs to the Dyer's Company.—This Company has, with the Vintner's Company, the right to keep swans on the Thames, each bird being marked with four bars and one nick; and the Vintner's birds are marked with the letter V and two nicks. Hence the tavern sign, "Swan with Two Necks."

EALING. A suburb of London, 6 miles by rail from Paddington.

EARL'S COURT EXHIBITIONS, with the Empress Theatre and Great Wheel.—Open every Season from May to October. Illuminated grounds, with bands, etc., in the evening, are a very attractive part of the entertainments here.

EDGWARE, MIDDLESEX.—A village about 8 miles from London. Edgware is said to have contained the blacksmith's shop that gave Handel the idea of the "Harmonius Blacksmith," and in Whitchurch, a short distance from Edgware, is the organ which Handel played on (1718-21). Rail from King's Cross, Great Northern Railway.

EDUCATIONAL MUSEUM at SOUTH KENSINGTON contains models of school buildings, scientific apparatus, etc.

EEL-PIE ISLAND. An island of seven acres, off Twickenham, close to the O leans Club. A fine view of Richmond Hill is obtained from it.

EGHAM. About 21 miles from Waterloo Station.—A small town, celebrated as being near Runnymede, supposed to be the spot where King John signed Magna Charta.

EGYPTIAN HALL, PICCADILLY.—Used principally for Maskelyne & Cook's clever Entertainment. Nearest Railway Station, St. James's Park.

ELECTRIC RAILWAYS. The City and South London Railway passes under the Thames to the Borough, "Elephant and Castle," Kennington Oval, on to Stockwell. The Waterloo & City Railway connects the City with the South Western Railway terminus and others, commencing at the Mansion House. The Central London Railway (opened in 1900) runs from the Bank of England Station, in front of the Royal Exchange, via Holborn, and Oxford Street, Marble Arch, Notting Hill Gate, to Shepherd's Bush.

"ELEPHANT AND CASTLE." A well known tavern near Newington Causeway. A halting station for omnibuses, etc. It is about a mile from Westminster, Waterloo, and Blackfriars Bridges.

THE NEIGHBOURHOOD OF SOUTH KENSINGTON (illustrated above) is noted for the The VICTORIA AND ALBERT (late the South Kensington) MUSEUM is one of the most int frontage shown in illustration being laid by Queen Victoria in 1899. The Imperial Institute, th part of the building is now converted to the use of the London University.

THE NATURAL HISTORY MUSEUM is a handsome new building to which the natural ▮ South-West Gallery, the animals, &c., are worth a visit.

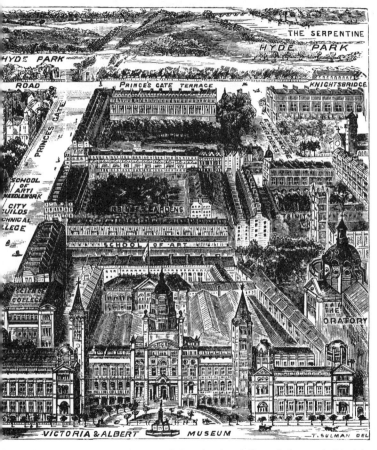

VICTORIA & ALBERT MUSEUM

T. SULMAN DEL

its institutions, Museums, and centres of educational, artistic, and also musical training.
ts for the visitor, and is at last being completed, the foundation-stone of the grand new
emorial of Queen Victoria's Jubilee, has only with partial success fulfilled its destiny, and

tions of the British Museum have been removed. The birds, admirably arranged in the

ELSTREE. A village in Hertfordshire, about 10 miles from London.—Good fishing may be obtained in the reservoir near.

ELTHAM. In KENT, about 8 miles from London.—Noted for its ancient Royal Palace.

EMIGRATION AGENTS for the Colonies:
CANADA.—17, Victoria Street, S.W.
CAPE OF GOOD HOPE.—98 and 100, Victoria Street, **S.W.**
NEW ZEALAND.—13, Victoria Street, S.W.
QUEENSLAND.—1, Victoria Street, S.W.
SOUTH AUSTRALIA.—28 to 31, Bishopsgate Street, E.C.
TASMANIA.—5, Victoria Street, S.W.
WESTERN AUSTRALIA.—15, Victoria Street, S.W.
OTHER COLONIES.—Colonial Office, Downing Street, **S.W.**

EMPIRE THEATRE. LEICESTER SQUARE.—Like the Alhambra, which is in the same Square, a large Music Hall, with the latest entertainments of the period.

ENFIELD. About 11 miles from Liverpool Street Station. Once the site of a Royal Palace; now known for the Government manufactory of small arms.

EPPING FOREST. Containing about 5,000 acres. Was purchased by the Corporation of London and opened by Queen Victoria in 1882 as a free public park and open space. It practically commences at Leyton, 6½ miles from Liverpool Street (G. E. Ry.), and reaches as far as Epping, 17 miles from the same station. Theydon Bois, Loughton, Buckhurst Hill, and Chigwell are on the eastern border of the Forest, and Chingford and High Beech on the western side. At Chingford the "Royal Forest Hotel" is situated, and the "King's Oak" is a well-known picnicing place at High Beech. Conveyances can be obtained at Chingford at moderate charges to enable visitors to get to the principal parts. The trees are very fine in many places, and the lover of nature will be delighted to revel through the green walks which are so frequent throughout the Forest. Cyclists abound here on all popular occasions and holidays, and as a place for a merry picnic it would be difficult to find any like Epping Fores', at least, near London.

EPSOM. A small town in Surrey, 18 miles from London. The Derby and Oaks are run on Epsom Downs yearly, about the last week in May.

ERITH. KENT.—On the right bank of the Thames, about 16 miles from London. The country behind it is very pretty and well wooded, affording many good walks in a pleasant part of Kent. Here are the headquarters of the Erith and Corinthian Yacht Clubs, and it is a favourite point for sailing matches.

ESHER. About 13 miles from Waterloo Station.—Sandown Park Races take place near here.

ETON. On the left bank of the Thames; from Oxford about 68½ miles, 43 miles from London.—Celebrated for Eton College, the greatest public school in England; founded 1441.

EUSTON STATION. In EUSTON ROAD.—The terminus of the London and North-Western Railway.

EVANS' SUPPER ROOMS were formerly situated in Covent Garden, in a building now occupied by the National Sporting Club.

EXCURSIONS.—The following are some of the places worth seeing near London:

BRIGHTON, sometimes called London-by-the-Sea, as so many Londoners live there About 50 miles from London. From London Bridge or Victoria (L. B. & S. C. R.).

BURNHAM BEECHES, in Buckinghamshire, about 20 miles from London.—Nearest Railway Station, Slough, thence by omnibus.

BUSHEY PARK, near Hampton Court Palace, about 12 miles from London.—Celebrated for its avenue of chestnut trees. Nearest Station, Teddington, from Waterloo.

CHATHAM.—Naval arsenal and military station on the Medway, about 30 miles from London.

CHISLEHURST, Kent, about 10 miles from London.—A picturesque Suburb.

CRYSTAL PALACE, Sydenham, about 7 miles from London.—This is the same building as used for the first Exhibition in Hyde Park in 1851. Frequent trains from Holborn, Victoria, and London Bridge.

DORKING, about 25 miles from London. Most lovely scenery, including Box Hill, and a splendid walk over Ranmore Common. The old coach road to Guildford (S.E.R.)

DULWICH.—In Dulwich College there is a fine Gallery of Pictures. Admission free.

EASTBOURNE.—Seaside on Sussex Coast, about 60 miles from London. One of our finest Southern watering places.

EPPING FOREST, Essex, 6 miles from London.—About 5,000 acres in extent. Beautiful walks, etc.

EPSOM, in Surrey, 12 miles from London.—The "Derby," and "Oaks," races are run here.

ERITH, on banks of the Thames, 16 miles from London.—A Yachting centre—regattas held here in summer.

ETON, Buckinghamshire, 20 miles from London, near Windsor.—Famous for the celebrated Eton School.

FOLKESTONE.—Seaside resort, 70 miles from London, on S.E. coast. A most charming place, full of life in the season. Shorncliffe military camp is near. A splendid line of steamers cross to Boulogne from here. A very healthy place; has good water, etc.

GRAVESEND, Kent, 30 miles from London.

GREENWICH, Kent, on bank of Thames, 4 miles from London Bridge.—The celebrated Seamen's Hospital and Royal Observatory are situated here: the Hospital contains a grand collection of naval pictures. Steamers from Old Swan Pier.

HAMPSTEAD HEATH. 6¾ miles from Broad Street.—One of the most picturesque open spaces near London, as Hampstead itself is one of its finest suburbs. Parliament Hill adjoins the Heath. A large estate, Golder's Hill has been lately added. From the summit of the Heath (marked by a flagstaff) a splendid view may be obtained of the country to the northwards, and of London southwards, if the day be clear.

HAMPTON COURT PALACE.—Founded by Cardinal Wolsey, and presented by him to Henry VIII. The state apartments were added in William III.'s reign, being designed by Sir Christopher Wren. These rooms are open to the public daily, except Friday, and contain interesting royal relics, a large collection of Italian and Dutch pictures, etc. The beautiful gardens, the long avenue of trees, the maze, and the celebrated grape vine make a visit here one of the many pleasant ones to be obtained round London. During the summer steamboats run from Old Swan Pier to and from Hampton Court. By rail from Waterloo or by Metropolitan and District Railways.

HARROW, Middlesex, 10 miles from London.—The celebrated Harrow Public School is here.

HASTINGS, Sussex, 60 miles from London, on S.E. coast.—A popular seaside place; especially mild in winter. St. Leonard's is a continuation of Hastings.

HATFIELD HOUSE, Herts, 18 miles from London.—The Marquis of Salisbury's residence.

HAYES, Kent, 12 miles from London.—Lord Chatham lived here.

KEW, Surrey, 9 miles from London.—Contains the celebrated Botanic Gardens, of about 70 acres; well worth a visit. From Waterloo (S.W.R.) or Metropolitan and District Railways,

KINGSTON-ON-THAMES, Surrey, on bank of Thames, 13 miles from London.—Good boating, etc.

[*Continued on page 54.*

EXCURSIONS—*continued.*

MARGATE.—Seaside resort, about 70 miles from London.—Very bracing air; very lively place; much frequented by Londoners of all sorts. In summer the large steamers of the "Palace," "Belle," and General Steam Navigation Companies run daily from London Bridge.

RICHMOND, Surrey, 9 miles from London.—A very popular riverside place. Good boating on the Thames, close to Richmond Park.

ROCHESTER, near Chatham.—Norman Castle and Cathedral.

RYE HOUSE, 19 miles from Liverpool Street Station.—The scene of the Rye House Plot. A place for excursionists.

ST. ALBANS, Herts, 21 miles from London.—This was the ancient Roman town of Verulamium; has fine Abbey, etc.

STOKE POGES, near Slough, 20 miles from London.—The churchyard here is that mentioned in Gray's "Elegy."

TWICKENHAM, Middlesex, on bank of Thames, 12 miles from London.—Orleans Club is here.

VIRGINIA WATER.—A charming artificial lake near Windsor.

WALTHAM ABBEY, Essex, 13 miles from London.—The Abbey was founded by King Harold.

WINDSOR, Berks, 22 miles from London.—Castle and Park are the great attractions here. Virginia Water is near.

WOOLWICH ARSENAL, on the right bank of the Thames, 7 miles from London.—Permits to look over the Arsenal can be obtained at the War Office.

EXETER HALL, 372, STRAND.—Is the property of the Young Men's Christian Association, and a large number of the "May Meetings," in aid of Christian and Philanthropic Societies, are held here. Devotional Addresses are constantly given, and Reading and Refreshment Rooms are attached. The large hall holds 5,000 people.

EXHIBITIONS. There have been many since the celebrated ones in 1851 and 1862, especially at Kensington. Earl's Court is open for the Season with all the popular elements of the Exhibition kind, including the Great Wheel, Illuminated Grounds, Music, etc.

FARRINGDON WITHIN AND WITHOUT, are two of the twenty-six wards of the City of London. Is the great newspaper publishing district, comprising Fleet Street, and its adjoining neighbourhoods.

FINSBURY PARK. HORNSEY.—Was opened in 1869 and cost £95,000; in extent it is about 100 acres (G.N.Ry. from King's Cross).

FIRE OF LONDON. The great Fire of 1666 commenced at the house of the "King's Baker," in Pudding Lane, and extended to Pye Corner, near Smithfield. Eighty-nine churches were burnt, about 13,200 dwelling houses, and 460 streets. It was said to be caused by a conspiracy of Papists, but this is now generally disbelieved.

FISHING. Full information with regard to fishing in the Thames will be found in the "Angler's Diary," published at the *Field* Office, price One Shilling and Sixpence.

FISHMONGER'S HALL is situated on the City end of LONDON BRIDGE.—Sir William Walworth, who slew Wat Tyler, was a member of this Company—one of the wealthiest of the City Companies.

FLAXMAN GALLERY. UNIVERSITY, GOWER STREET.—The Hall under the dome and other apartments are adorned by works of the late John Flaxman, Professor of Sculpture. Public admitted on Saturdays in May, June, July, and August, from 10 a.m. to 4 p.m.

FLEET (THE) was once an open stream of water, taking its rise at Hampstead, and came through Kentish Town and Camden Town to Fleet Street—now covered over.

FLEET PRISON stood on the east side of FARRINGDON STREET; was pulled down in 1846. This was a most interesting prison, on account of the many eminent persons confined there; many of whom died there. As clergymen were often sent there for debt, they used to marry persons in the Chapel attached, without license or other usual formalities, and such marriages were legally binding. This was stopped in 1711; but after this the marriages took place in the taverns near, but this scandal was stopped in 1774.

THE THAMES EMBANKMENT.

HE VICTORIA EMBANKMENT extends along left bank of the Thames, from Westminster Bridge to Blackfriars Bridge, about a mile and a quarter. Adjoining and facing the Embankment are Somerset House, The Temple, Adelphi Terrace, St. Stephen's Club, National Liberal Club, School Board House, and City of London School. On the river wall is erected the celebrated Cleopatra Needle, which was one of the two obelisks which stood before the great temple of Heliopolis, near the site of modern Alexandria.

FLEET STREET (leads from LUDGATE HILL to the STRAND) is one of the most well known streets in London. It contains many places of interest, and is the centre of the Newspaper trade. *The Daily Telegraph* has an imposing building in this street, whilst most of the great dailies are published in or near it. Cook's Tourist Offices are at the corner of Ludgate Circus.

FOREIGN MONEY EXCHANGED at Cook's Tourist Offices, Ludgate Circus, 445, Strand; 33, Piccadilly; 82, Oxford Street; 13, Cockspur Street; and in the City at the corner of Gracechurch Street.

FOREIGN OFFICE. DOWNING STREET, S.W. part of the large Public Offices.— Building designed by the late Sir Gilbert Scott. Receptions are sometimes given here by the Minister for Foreign Affairs.

FOUNDLING HOSPITAL. GUILDFORD STREET, W.C.—One of the most interesting Charities in London, and every one should go and see it. Founded in 1739 by the gentle-hearted Captain Thomas Coram, with the object of feeding, clothing, and educating litt'e children in destitute circumstances. These may be seen every Sunday at the morning servi e in the large Chapel attached to the Home. Strangers are admitted on payment of a small offering at the doors. The music and singing are very beautiful. After church visitors can see the children at dinner; also they can see over a handsome suite of apartments containing many great curiosities, including some very celebrated pictures by Reynolds, Gainsborough, Hogarth, Wilson, etc. The very youngest children are kept in another house in the country. Sunday service at 11 a.m. Nearest Railway Station, King's Cross.

FREEDOM OF THE CITY OF LONDON is obtained *By servitude*—that is, being bound as an apprentice to a Freeman for 7 years: *By patrimony*—viz., being the son of a Freeman; *By gift of the City*; or *By purchase*.

FREEMASONS' HALL. GREAT QUEEN STREET.—The centre of English Free-masonry, where are the offices of Grand Lodge and Grand Chapter, and where the meetings of these governing bodies of the Freemasons take place. The Masonic Schools for Girls are at St. John's Hill, Battersea Rise, and for Boys at Wood Green, N.

FULHAM. A suburb of London, on the banks of the Thames, opposite Putney. The old Palace of Fulham is the residence of the Bishop of London. The old part of the building dates from the 14th century. Hurlingham House, Fulham, is well known for pigeon shooting and other sports.

FURNIVALS' INN. HOLBORN.—Formerly an Inn of Chancery, then used as Chambers; now pulled down to make room for the Prudential Insurance Company's Offices. Charles Dickens wrote "Pickwick Papers" in his chambers here.

GADSHILL, near ROCHESTER, is where Charles Dickens resided and died in 1870.

GAIETY THEATRE. STRAND.—A handsomely decorated, good-sized house. Nearest Railway Station, Temple. Devoted to Burlesque and Extravaganza.

GARDENS.—See Botanic Gardens, Chelsea Botanic Gardens, Kew Gardens, North Woolwich Gardens, Kensington Gardens, Royal Horticultural Gardens, Zoological Gardens, etc.

GARRICK CLUB, 13 and 15, GARRICK STREET, COVENT GARDEN.—Dates from 1831. A Literary and Theatrical Club-house, containing a large collection of interesting portraits of actors, etc.

THE HOUSES OF PARLIAMENT.

THE HOUSES OF PARLIAMENT are situated close to Westminster Bridge, and the House of Peers and the House of Commons, also the grand and interesting Westminster Hall, which is very old and connected with many interesting historical associations. In this Hall were held the very early English Parliaments; here Charles I. was condemned to death, also the Earl of Strafford. The Clock Tower contains the large bell called Big Ben, which weighs thirteen tons, and can be heard over a large part of London. The Houses of Parliament can be seen on Saturdays, gratis between 10 and 4.

GARRICK THEATRE. CHARING CROSS ROAD, near National Gallery.—Was opened April 24th, 1889.

GENERAL POST OFFICE. ST. MARTIN'S-LE-GRAND.—The imposing buildings at the end of Aldersgate Street form the centre of the postal system in England. The old building on the right was built in 1829, and is the head office of the London Postal District. Although added to by the addition of another floor, it is overshadowed by the building immediately opposite, which contains the Telegraph Department. Next to this huge building is another lately constructed, still more extensive, in which are the offices of the Postmaster-General and the Accountant-General, the Solicitor, the Secretary. and their staffs, etc.

GENERAL STEAM NAVIGATION CO., 55, GREAT TOWER STREET, E.C., and 14, WATERLOO PLACE, S.W.—One of the large companies who cater for the sea-loving public, their steamboats running daily during the summer season to Margate and Ramsgate, Southend and Yarmouth, from London Bridge Wharf. See Newspapers for Times and Fares.

GEOLOGICAL MUSEUM. JERMYN STREET, PICCADILLY. — Contains a superb collection of minerals, metals, etc. Open free, except on Fridays. On Monday and Saturday evenings the Museum is illuminated with the electric light until 10 p.m.

"GEORGE AND BLUE BOAR" was an Inn situated at 285, HIGH HOLBORN, and used to be the last house of call for refreshment by criminals on their way to Tyburn to be hanged, and had in other respects an historical interest.

GOG AND MAGOG. Traditional City giants. Two large figures in the Guildhall establish their identity.

GOLDSMITHS' HALL. FOSTER LANE, CHEAPSIDE, in rear of General Post Office.— Was opened in 1835. The Goldsmiths are a very ancient guild, and date from 1180—perhaps before. Were incorporated in 1327. Silver and gold plate are "Hall-stamped" here.

GORING. OXFORDSHIRE.—On the left bank of the Thames. Is 45 miles from Paddington, on G.W.R., and situated in the midst of picturesque scenery; is much resorted to in the summer for fishing, boating, and picnic parties.

GOVERNMENT OFFICES. WHITEHALL.—The extensive buildings erected in 1876, containing the Home, Colonial, India, and Foreign Offices, were designed by Sir Gilbert Scott, and with the Treasury Offices adjoining, and the new buildings to be erected in Parliament Street, will form a splendid series of public buildings.

GRAVESEND. KENT.—On the right bank of the Thames, 27 miles from London. A station on the North Kent Railway, 24 miles by rail from Charing Cross. Owing to its position, is considered the gateway of the Port of London. Outward-bound ships take pilots here, and homeward Custom officers.

GRAY'S INN In HOLBORN.—An Inn of Court, named after Lord Gray de Wilton, of Henry VII.'s reign. A fine Elizabethan hall built in 1560; is notable for its fine wood carving. Shakespeare's "Comedy of Errors" was acted here in 1594.

GRAYS THUROCK.—A small town on the left (Essex) bank of the Thames, about 23 miles by river from London Bridge.

GREAT CENTRAL RAILWAY. MARYLEBONE, W.—This new terminus in London is fronted by a huge hotel in the Marylebone Road. The line proceeds *via* Aylesbury to Rugby, Leicester, Nottingham, Sheffield. Manchester, and Liverpool.

GREAT EASTERN RAILWAY. LIVERPOOL STREET, E.C.—Connects Cambridge, Colchester, Harwich, Ipswich, Norwich, Yarmouth, etc., with London.

Service to the Continent, via Harwich to the Hook of Holland and Rotterdam, daily, Sundays included; Antwerp every week-day, Hamburg twice weekly, and Denmark three times a week; also the Cathedral Route for American passengers between Liverpool and London.

GREAT MARLOW. BUCKINGHAMSHIRE.—On the left bank of River Thames, by rail 35 miles from Paddington. Much frequented for fishing, boating, and holiday purposes.

GRECIAN THEATRE. CITY ROAD.—Purchased by "General" Booth, Salvation Army.

GREENHITHE.—A village on the Thames, about 20 miles from Charing Cross Station Some training ships lie here; it is also a yachting station.

GREEN PARK.—Contains about 60 acres. It contains the carriage track near Buckingham Palace, called Constitution Hill, where Sir Robert Peel was thrown from his horse and killed, 1850.

TRAFALGAR SQUARE.

TRAFALGAR SQUARE is one of the finest open spaces in London. Contains several statues, the most important being Nelson's Monument, erected to commemorate his death at the battle of Trafalgar, Oct. 22, 1805. By this victory Napoleon's purpose of invading England was frustrated. A statue to the late revered General Gordon is erected here. On the north side of the Square is the National Gallery.

GREENWICH HOSPITAL AND ROYAL NAVAL COLLEGE. GREENWICH, S.E.—
Well worth a visit. The Painted Hall contains some fine pictures of sea-fights. The most interesting of the Greenwich sights, however, are the relics of Nelson, notably the Trafalgar Coat and Waistcoat. Admission free from 7 a.m. to 5 p.m., and on Sundays from 1 p.m. The Painted Hall and Naval Museum are open to the public every week-day excepting Fridays at 10 a.m. to 4 p.m.; the Painted Hall is open on Sundays at 2 p.m.

GREENWICH PARK.—Immediately adjoins Greenwich Hospital, and is a beautiful spot, and well worth a visit. Greenwich Observatory is where the Astronomer Royal conducts his observations, and gives "Greenwich Time" to all the world.

GROCERS' HALL is situated in the POULTRY.—The Grocers' Company was incorporated in 1345.

GROSVENOR BRIDGE.—A handsome railway bridge over the Thames at Victoria Station.

GROSVENOR HOUSE, UPPER GROSVENOR STREET, is the Town residence of the Duke of Westminster. Contains a grand and valuable collection of pictures.

GROSVENOR SQUARE is a very fashionable place of residence for many prominent members of the aristocracy.

GUILDHALL (THE), KING STREET, CHEAPSIDE.—The Hall of the City Corporation was originally built in the 15th Century, was damaged by the Great Fire in 1666, then restored and a new frontage built in 1789, with the exception of the porch, which is part of the original building. It is used for municipal business—Election of Lord Mayor and great public meetings on matters of National and Social interest. The banquet following the Lord Mayor's procession to the Law Courts on his taking office on the 9th November in each year is held here, at which the Prime Minister and other members of the Government are present, and during which important public announcements are often made. The Hall itself has a fine roof, erected by Sir Horace Jones in 1865, stained glass windows, one in memory of Prince Albert, and large monuments in honour of Earl Chatham, William Pitt, Nelson, and Wellington. Lady Jane Grey, executed in the Tower, was tried in this Hall. Adjoining are the Aldermen's Room and the Common Council Chamber, the latter designed by Sir Horace Jones, and built in 1885. The Corporation Free Library is also connected with Guildhall, admission free daily from 10 to 4 or 5, and the Museum adjoining, with many objects of ancient interest connected with the Metropolis. There is also an Art Gallery, and a Special Annual Free Exhibition of Great Works of Art has been of late years held here in the spring.

GWYNNE (NELL) was buried in the Crypt of St. Martin's Church, Trafalgar Square. She was acting at Drury Theatre in 1666; she lived at 79, Pall Mall, from 1670 to 1687, when she died. It is reported that it was by her influence that the Chelsea Hospital for old soldiers was founded by Charles II., whose favourite she was.

HABERDASHERS' HALL, 33, GRESHAM STREET, behind GENERAL POST OFFICE.—Contains portraits of eminent Haberdashers. The Company maintain several Schools.

HACKNEY.—A suburb of London, including Upper and Lower Clapton; is said to have given its name to the first Hackney coaches.

HAMBLEDON, BUCKS, on the left bank of the Thames, about 62 miles from London by the river. Near here is Greenlands, the seat of the late Right Hon. W. H. Smith, M.P.

HAMMERSMITH.—A suburb of London, on the banks of the Thames. *A branch of Chas. Baker & Co.'s Stores will be found at* 27, 29, 31 *and* 33, *King Street, Broadway.*

HAMPSTEAD HEATH.—A stretch of real country within easy reach of the heart of London, one of the few spots as yet unspoiled by improvement. It lies high above the Cross of St. Paul's. A large estate, Golder's Hill, has recently been added to the Heath.

HAMPTON COURT PALACE.—This splendid Palace was built by Cardinal Wolsey, in 1515, and afterwards presented to King Henry VIII. in 1526. Henry VIII. passed a good deal of his time at this Palace. Here Edward VI. was born, and Jane Seymour died; and here the King was married to his sixth wife, Katharine Parr. It was a favourite residence of Charles I. and Cromwell. William III. considerably enlarged and altered the Palace, and had the gardens and park laid out as they now appear. Its last royal occupant was George II. The State Apartments, Picture Galleries, Gardens, Maze, and large Grape-vine are well worth seeing. Bushey Park is also near, with its splendid avenue of chestnut trees. The Palace is open to the public free every day, except Fridays and Christmas day. Hours, 10 to 4; Sundays from 2 p.m. Visitors can go by Rail from Waterloo Station; also by Steamboat. Electric Trams, Omnibus, etc.

HANWELL.—A village about 7 miles by rail from London. It has a large lunatic asylum.

HARROW-ON-THE-HILL.—Noted for its great School, competing with Eton amongst the highest public Schools of England. Lord Byron, the poet, was a pupil here, and many other notable people, including the statesmen Peel and Palmerston. The spire of Harrow Church, situated on the famous Hill, is a conspicuous object for miles around, and stands out prominently in the view from Hampstead Heath. Trains from Euston, and Metropolitan Railway from Baker Street.

HARLEY STREET, CAVENDISH SQUARE, is largely occupied by physicians, etc.

HASTINGS AND ST. LEONARDS.—A beautiful watering place, with a mild climate, especially adapted for invalids. Hot in summer, but genial in winter, with a fine sea and pier. About 60 miles from London (C. & S.E.R. and L.B. & S.C.R.).

HATCHAM.—A suburb of London, near New Cross.

HATTON GARDEN is a street leading from HOLBORN CIRCUS; so called from being built on the garden of Hatton House. Used to be a fashionable place of private residence; is now largely used by diamond merchants.

HAYES, KENT, 12 miles from London.—Lord Chatham lived here.

HAYMARKET (THE), a street leading from PALL MALL, is noted as being for many years the centre of the late-hour life of the West End. The old Haymarket Theatre, so long under the management of Mr. Buckstone, was reconstructed by Mr. (now Sir Squire) Bancroft, and was for some years under the management of himself and his popular wife (once Miss Marie Wilton). Mr. Tree succeeded as lessee, and he has now removed to the new Theatre, His Majesty's, opposite, close to which is the great Hotel, the "Carlton," one of the modern public palaces of London. The Haymarket Theatre is still open for good-class Comedies, etc., under new and successful management.

HAYMARKET THEATRE (see above).

HENDON. About 7 miles from London, near Finchley.—Here is situated the "Welsh Harp," a place of holiday resort for Londoners. The lake at Hendon is well-known to anglers and skaters.

HENLEY ROYAL REGATTA.—This favourite event takes place usually about the beginning of July. The course is a little over a mile and a quarter in length, and the races are rowed from Regatta Island, just below Remenham, against the stream, to a point opposite the "Red Lion" and just below the bridge. It is considered the most important of the Thames Regattas, and crews from the leading London clubs and the Universities compete. It is largely attended, and the view of the crowded river at Regatta time is extremely animated and glows with bright colours.

HERALD'S COLLEGE OF ARMS is in QUEEN VICTORIA STREET, E.C.—Contains many objects of interest to antiquaries. Armorial bearings are issued from here.

HERTFORD HOUSE, MANCHESTER SQUARE. (See Wallace Collection.)—Open free Monday, Wednesday, Thursday, and Saturday; Monday at 12 a.m., other days 10 a.m.; Tuesday and Friday on payment of 6d. Closes January 4 p.m., February 4.30 p.m., March 5 p.m., April to September 6 p.m., October 5 p.m., November and December 4 p.m.; Sundays open only from April to October inclusive; from 2 p.m. to 5 in April and October; from 2 to 6, May to September.

HERTFORD. An interesting old town near London, situated on south bank of River Lea. Contains remains of two castles; near here are several handsome country seats, especially Hatfield House, the residence of the Marquis of Salisbury.

HIGH BARNET is about 11 miles from London by rail. At Hadley, near here, the Battle of Barnet was fought in 1471, when the Earl of Warwick was slain; this was the last conflict but one between the Red and White Roses. Hadley Woods are a favourite spot for picnics, etc.

HIGHBURY.—A residential suburb of London, near Islington.

HIGHGATE.—One of the Northern heights of London; still retains much of its old-world appearance, although like all other suburbs being attacked by the demon builder. The spire of the Parish Church overlooking the Cemetery is a conspicuous object for many miles. Has many old residential houses and a large Public School. Highgate Woods (close to Highgate Station, G.N.R.), bought by the Corporation of London for the people are delightful; so also is the Queen's Wood, quite adjacent, opened by the Duchess of Albany, and under the charge of the Hornsey District Council.

HOLBORN, a continuation of Oxford Street towards the City, being situated on high ground, with good gravel soil, is very healthy; as it is midway between the West End and the City, it is a good part of London for strangers to stay   The principal Hotels are "The Inns of Court" and "The First Avenue," the latter being one of the Gordon Hotels.—**The** "Holborn Restaurant," truly one of the sights of London, should be visited as a matter of course. It represents the height of modern comfort and luxury, whether one goes for an ordinary luncheon or to the Table d'Hote in the Grand Salon in the evening, where music is rendered. The King's Hall is certainly one of the finest of its kind in London, and with other large rooms is much used for public Dinners, Balls, etc.—The Birkbeck Bank has a new and handsome frontage in Holborn, close to the old houses of Staples Inn, and nearly opposite are the immense buildings of the Prudential Assurance Company. On one side of Holborn is the Inn of Court called Gray's Inn, whilst on the opposite side leading to the Law Courts and the Strand is Lincoln's Inn, with large Hall and Grounds. Lincoln's Inn Fields are open free to the public under the London County Council.—The business houses in Holborn best known are probably Thomas Wallis & Co., the large drapers, and the Head Depot of Chas. Baker & Co., next door to the Inns of Court Hotel, the large tailors, clothiers, and outfitters, who have also several branches in London. *(See Price List at end of Book.)*

HOUNDSDITCH.—The quarter for old clothes and second-hand dealers, principally Jewish.

HOUNSLOW.—A town about 13 miles from Charing Cross Station. Hounslow Heath was the site of an encampment by the forces of James II. after Sedgmoor, and was noted for highwaymen in the eighteenth century.

HOLBORN CIRCUS is situated between HOLBORN VIADUCT and HOLBORN; in the centre is a statue of Prince Albert, the father of King Edward VII.

HOLBORN VIADUCT connects HOLBORN with NEWGATE STREET; was built across the Fleet Valley to get rid of the steep Holborn and Snow Hills. It was opened by Queen Victoria in 1869. Here is the Holborn Terminus of the S.E. & C. Railway.

HOLLOWAY.—A large suburban district between Highbury and Highgate; the Holloway Road ending at the Archway Tavern. SPECIAL NOTICE.—*A large branch of Chas. Baker & Co.'s Stores for Tailoring, Clothing, and Outfitting is open in this district at 5, 7 & 9, Seven Sisters Road, opposite the "Nag's Head."*

HOLLOWAY COLLEGE (THE ROYAL).—Founded in 1883 by the late Mr. Thomas Holloway, proprietor of the well-known Pills and Ointment, is situated at Mount Lee, Egham, Surrey; is built in the style of the French Renaissance; its object is to supply the most suitable education for women of the middle and upper middle-classes. Residence is ordinarily restricted to three years, but the governors have power to admit non-resident students. The fees are uniform for all residents. The first board of management included the Archbishop of Canterbury and Earl Granville. The building was opened by the Queen in 1886, and contains a collection of pictures by Millais, Landseer, Frith, Constable, and other eminent artists.

HOLYWELL STREET, STRAND.—Was a narrow side street, chiefly occupied by second-hand booksellers; it was named from an old well supposed to have been situated under a tavern here, and has now been entirely swept away for the widening of the Strand.

HOME OFFICE.—Part of the Public Offices designed by Sir Gilbert Scott in Whitehall, erected in 1873.

HONOURABLE ARTILLERY COMPANY have their extensive Armoury and Parade-ground near Bunhill Fields; the corps is said to have been incorporated by Henry VIII. in 1537.

HORSE GUARDS, WHITEHALL.—Has Life-Guardsmen as sentinels during the day in the two sentry boxes each side of the entrance. The passage under the Clock Tower leads to St. James's Park and Buckingham Palace. At the Horse Guards Parade the ceremony of Trooping the Colours on the King's Birthday is held.

HORSLEYDOWN, SOUTHWARK.—Extends from TOOLEY STREET to DOCKHEAD. Was so called from being formerly used as grazing ground for horses.

HORTICULTURAL SOCIETY (ROYAL).—The Gardens are at South Kensington and Chiswick. Members' Tickets, 1, 2, and 4 Guineas.

HOSPITALS.—London abounds with these and kindred institutions for the relief of poor people. The principal Central Hospitals are Guy's, St. Bartholomew's and St. Thomas's, but a complete list will be found in Kelly's Post Office London Directory.

HOUSES OF PARLIAMENT, WESTMINSTER.—One of the finest and largest

Gothic buildings in the world. Covers 8 acres of ground. The River Facade is 940 feet in length. Completed in 1857 at a cost of £3,000,000, the architect being Sir Charles Barry. On this site stood the old Royal Palace of Westminster. Westminster Hall was built by William Rufus, and King Stephen added a magnificent Chapel dedicated to the martyr, hence the name St. Stephen's frequently applied to the House of Commons. The Palace was burnt early in the 16th Century and Westminster ceased to be a royal residence, but the Chapel continued to be the meeting place of the Commons until 1834. The most striking architectural features of the Parliament Houses are the two great towers, the Victoria Tower (the height to the top of the flagstaff being 420 feet) and the St. Stephen's, or Clock Tower (316 feet high). The latter contains the huge bell, "Big Ben," which weighs about 14 tons. When Parliament is sitting an electric light burns at the summit of St. Stephen's Tower, or in daylight a Union Jack flies on the Victoria Tower.—The interior can be viewed on any Saturday throughout the year from 10 to 3.30, entering by the *Victoria Tower* to the King's *Robing Room* and the *Royal Gallery*, through which the King passes to the House of Lords when opening Parliament. In this gallery are two fine frescoes by Maclise, "The Death of Nelson" and "The Meeting of Wellington and Blucher after Waterloo." The visitor then passes through the beautiful *Princes Chamber* to the House of Lords, a truly magnificent chamber, where is the throne under a rich canopy, then through the Corridor to the *Central Hall*, through the Commons Lobby to the House of Commons with Speaker's Chair, etc., and out of the buildings by way of Westminster Hall. When you have seen the chambers and corridors, the latter richly decorated with frescoes and statuary, you will be prepared to admit that these fine buildings are worthy of the Victorian Era, in which so much has been done to add to the liberty and the improvement of the people, without interfering with the constitutional and continuous form of Government so suited to the English race. (See also Westminster Hall, farther on in book.)

HOTELS.—The following are some of the best known Hotels :—
ALEXANDRA HOTEL, St. George's Place, Hyde Park Corner.
ANDERTON'S HOTEL, 162, Fleet Street.
BUCKINGHAM PALACE HOTEL, Buckingham Palace Gate.
CANNON STREET HOTEL, Cannon Street Station.
CARLTON HOTEL, Haymarket (corner of the).
CHARING CROSS HOTEL, Charing Cross Station.
DE KEYSER'S ROYAL HOTEL, Victoria Embankment, Blackfriars.
EUSTON HOTEL, Euston Station.
FIRST AVENUE HOTEL, High Holborn.
GOLDEN CROSS HOTEL, Strand, opposite Charing Cross Station.
GRAND HOTEL, Charing Cross.
GREAT CENTRAL RAILWAY HOTEL, Marylebone Road.
GREAT EASTERN HOTEL, Liverpool Street Station.
GREAT NORTHERN RAILWAY HOTEL, King's Cross Station.
GREAT WESTERN HOTEL, Paddington Station.
GROSVENOR HOTEL, Victoria Station, Pimlico.
HOLBORN VIADUCT HOTEL, Holborn Viaduct Station.
HOTEL CECIL, Strand and Thames Embankment.
HOTEL METROPOLE, Northumberland Avenue.
HOTEL RUSSELL, Russell Square.
HOTEL VICTORIA, Northumberland Avenue.
HOTEL WINDSOR, Victoria Street, Westminster.
HUMMUM'S HOTEL, Covent Garden.
INNS OF COURT HOTEL, High Holborn, with entrance from Lincoln's Inn Fields.
LANGHAM HOTEL, Portland Place.
MANCHESTER HOTEL, Aldersgate Street.
METROPOLITAN HOTEL, Moorgate Street, near Great Eastern Station.
MIDLAND RAILWAY HOTEL, St. Pancras Station, Euston Road.
SALISBURY HOTEL, Salisbury Square.
SAVOY HOTEL, Thames Embankment.
TERMINUS HOTEL, London Bridge Station.
WESTMINSTER PALACE HOTEL, Victoria Street, Westminster.
The above are large Hotels. There are also a number of good middle-class Hotels, comfortable, with moderate charges. The following are some of the central addresses :—

HOTELS—*continued.*

ADELPHI HOTEL, 1 to 4, John Street, Adelphi, W.C.
ARMFIELD'S HOTEL, South Place, Finsbury, E.C.
ARUNDEL HOTEL, Arundel Street, Strand, W.C.
BINGHAM HOTEL, Southampton Buildings, Chancery Lane.
BUCKINGHAM HOTEL (Temperance), 28, Buckingham Street, Strand.
CALEDONIAN HOTEL, Adelphi Terrace, W.C.
GOWER HOTEL (THE), close to Gower Street Station, Euston Road.
HAXELL'S HOTEL, 369 to 375, Strand, W.C.
HORREX'S HOTEL, corner of Norfolk Street, Strand.
HOWARD HOTEL, Norfolk Street, Strand.
KENNAN'S HOTEL, 3, Crown Court, Cheapside.
KENT'S HOTEL, 32, Norfolk Street, Strand.
LAY'S HOTEL, 5 to 9, Surrey Street, Strand.
LOUDOUN HOTEL, 21, Surrey Street, Strand.
MANDEVILLE HOTEL, 8 and 10, Mandeville Place, W.
MULLIN'S HOTEL, Ironmonger Lane, E.C.
NORFOLK HOTEL, 30 to 32, Surrey Street, Strand.
RAYMENT'S HOTEL, 18 and 19, London Wall, E.C.
SARACEN'S HEAD HOTEL, 10, Snow Hill, Holborn.
SUTTIE'S HOTEL, 24 to 27, Bedford Place, W.C.
TRANTER'S HOTEL (Temperance), 6, 7, 8 and 9, Bridgwater Square, E.C.
WAVERLEY HOTEL (Cranston's), Southampton Row, W.C.
WALDUCK'S BEDFORD HOTEL, 91 to 95, Southampton Row, W.C.
WEST CENTRAL TEMPERANCE HOTELS, 75, etc., Southampton Row, W.C.
WILD'S TEMPERANCE HOTEL, 34 to 40, Ludgate Hill, E.C.
WILLIAMSON's HOTEL, 1 to 3, New Court, Bow Lane, E.C.

PRIVATE HOTELS (not licensed). A complete list of these can be found in *Kelly's Post Office London Directory*, from which the following are taken:—

ANDREW'S HOTEL, 68, Guildford Street, W.C.
BARNETT'S HOTEL, 37 and 39, Craven Street, Strand.
BARTLETT'S HOTEL, 12, Upper Woburn Place, W.C.
BERNARD'S HOTEL, 1, 2, 3 and 4, Granville Square, W.C.
BONN'S HOTEL, 1, Craven Street, Strand.
BROWN'S HOTEL, 3 and 4, Craven Street, Strand.
COLLISON'S HOTEL, 28 to 34, Wigmore Street, W.
CRANSTON'S WAVERLEY HOTELS, 132, Southampton Row, and 37, King Street, E.C.
DANIEL'S HOTEL, 9 and 10, Thavie's Inn, Holborn.
DAVEY'S HOTEL, 66, Guildford Street, W.C.
DONKIN'S HOTEL, 8 and 9, Grenville Street, Brunswick Square, W.C.
DUNN'S HOTEL, 19 and 20, Woburn Place, W.C.
FORSTER'S HOTEL, 21, Woburn Place, W.C.
GUTHRIE'S HOTEL, 69, Guildford Street, W.C.
KINGSLEY HOTEL, 36, 37 and 38, Hart Street, Bloomsbury, W.C.
KLEIN'S HOTEL, 38, Finsbury Square, E.C.
MASON'S HOTEL, 18, 19 and 20, Montague Street, W.C.
MEGGY'S HOTEL, 42, Craven Street, Strand.
MERRITT'S HOTEL, 14, Upper Woburn Place, W.C.
MIDLAND TEMPERANCE HOTEL, 74, 75 and 76, Guildford Street, W.C.
MONTAGUE MANSIONS HOTEL, 52, Russell Street, W.C.
POER'S HOTEL, 107, Great Russell Street, W.C.
PRIVETT'S HOTEL, 24, Southampton Row, W.C.
RICHARDSON'S HOTEL, 38, Craven Street, Strand.
RUTTER'S HOTEL, 29 and 31, Queen Square, W.C.
TAVERNER'S HOTEL, 41 and 43, Judd Street, W.C.
THACKERAY HOTEL, Great Russell Street, W.C.
TRUSLOVE'S HOTEL, 1, Montague Street, Russell Square, W.C.
TURNER'S HOTEL, 74, 75 and 76, Guildford Street, W.C.
WILLIAMS'S HOTEL, 2 and 3, Montague Street, W.C.

The above private Hotels are given principally for the West Central District. Others will be added, if requested, in future editions.

HOXTON.—A populous suburb adjoining SHOREDITCH. It has a large theatre called the Britannia.

HYDE PARK.—This is by far the most favourite and fashionable park in London. With Kensington Gardens, which is a continuation, it covers over 630 acres. The popular entrances to the park are at Hyde Park Corner, at the end of Piccadilly (where, in the season, the long drive is crowded in the afternoons between 5 and 7), and the Marble Arch, close to Edgware Road, at the end of Oxford Street. The flower gardens are well kept in the spaces opposite Park Lane, and Rotten Row is supplemented with a fine display of Rhododendrons, etc., in the early summer. The Serpentine runs almost across the Park, on which boating, and in which, at appointed times, bathing, are permitted. The Achilles Monument, inside the park from Hyde Park Corner, is in memory of "the great Duke and his companions in arms," and Apsley House, the residence of the Duke of Wellington, is close to that entrance. Further on is the Albert Memorial and Albert Hall, leading to the Museums. (For KENSINGTON GARDENS and PALACE, see farther on in book.)

IMPERIAL INSTITUTE, SOUTH KENSINGTON.—Open free to the public daily (Sundays excepted) from 11 a.m. to dusk. Was intended as a national memorial of the completion of the fiftieth year of Queen Victoria's reign. The foundation stone was laid by Queen Victoria in 1887, and it was opened by Her Majesty, in great state, on May 10th, 1893. *(See illustration on pages 50 and 51.)* Was intended as a centre for information and consultation on all matters connected with the Empire, but has not altogether succeeded in that purpose. It has now been taken over by the Board of Trade.

INDIAN MUSEUM.—Forms part of the South Kensington—now the Victoria and Albert—Museum.

INDIA OFFICE, ST. JAMES'S SQUARE.—From here the affairs of our Indian Empire are regulated by the Secretary of State for India, whose official salary is £5,000 per annum.

INLAND REVENUE OFFICE, SOMERSET HOUSE, STRAND.—Is very large, and has many branches in this vast building.

INNS OF COURT.—Four in number, viz., Inner Temple, Middle Temple, Lincoln's Inn, and Gray's Inn. The Inns consist of a hall, chapel, library, a suite of rooms devoted to the benchers, and sets of chambers for barristers and solicitors.

INSTITUTE OF PAINTERS IN WATER COLOURS (ROYAL), PICCADILLY GALLERIES, 191, PICCADILLY.—Open from Easter to June. Admission, 1s.

INSTITUTION OF CIVIL ENGINEERS, 25, GREAT GEORGE STREET, WESTMINSTER.—Was incorporated in 1828.

IRONMONGERS' HALL is situated on the North side of FENCHURCH STREET, opposite MARK LANE. Contains several interesting portraits.

ISLE OF DOGS.—On the river, between Limehouse and Blackwall. Nearest Steamboat Pier, Millwall.

ISLEWORTH, MIDDLESEX.—On the left bank of the Thames. Distance from London, 15 miles by water; 12 miles from Waterloo by rail. Here is the last lock on the River.

ISLINGTON, one of the large parishes, and, for the future, one of the many corporate boroughs, of London, extends from "The Angel" to Highgate Archway, has a population of nearly 350,000, and sends four members to Parliament.—The Agricultural Hall, used for the Cattle Show in December, the Royal Military Tournament in the spring, and for numerous trade exhibitions, etc., during the year, is in Upper Street.

JACK STRAW'S CASTLE.—A well-known old inn on Hampstead Heath. Jack Straw commanded a division of the insurgents under Wat Tyler. It is mentioned in Fosters "Life of Dicken's": the famous novelist visited it.

JACOB'S ISLAND is situated near ROTHERHITHE.—This island is mentioned by Dickens in "Oliver Twist."

JEWISH SYNAGOGUES.—There are more than sixty in London; the Central one is at 129, Great Portland Street, W.

JEWRY (OLD) was named by the Jews dwelling there; it leads out of Cheapside.

KEMPTON PARK, near SUNBURY, MIDDLESEX.—On the left bank of the Thames; is the Racecourse constructed by the Kempton Park Club. The distance from London by water is 26½ miles; by rail, to Sunbury Station, 15½ miles from Waterloo.

KENNINGTON OVAL.—The County Ground of the Surrey Cricket Club, and where most of the London matches of that Club are played. One of the sights of London when a big match is being played with some competing county or by the Australians when visiting England. At least 20,000 people, mostly men, are to be seen watching these matches with all the interest and enthusiasm cricket excites in Englishmen. Nearest route from the City, by Electric Railway, or by 'Bus from Ludgate Circus or Charing Cross.

KENNINGTON PARK.—A square, containing about 12 acres, in the South of London. Nearest Railway Station, Walworth Road.

KENSINGTON, near HYDE PARK.—Is a fashionable place of residence.

KENSINGTON GARDENS, with its pleasant walks and fine trees and flower gardens, skirting the Serpentine, is a continuation of Hyde Park.—At the extreme west are the Round Pond (used for early skating in winter) and Kensington Palace, in front of which is a statue of Queen Victoria by the Princess Louise.

KENSINGTON PALACE.—An old building in Queen Anne style. William and Mary and Queen Anne lived here. It is specially interesting to the people of this era as being the birthplace of Queen Victoria, and where she was apprised of the death of her uncle, William IV., and of her accession to the throne. The State rooms are now thrown open to the public.

KENTISH TOWN is situated between CAMDEN TOWN and HIGHGATE.—At no very remote time both Camden and Kentish Towns were country villages, but now are populous and busy parts of the Metropolis.

KEW GARDENS.—One of the most favourite resorts near London. Houses for tropical palms and plants, ferns and flowers, with Botanical Museums and beautiful grounds and walks. The Pagoda is at one end of the Gardens. Open from 10 until sunset daily. Sunday, opened at 1. Kew Palace adjoins, the grounds of which are now added to the Gardens. Rail from Waterloo; also by Metropolitan and District Railways, and Electric Trams from Shepherd's Bush.

KING'S COLLEGE, STRAND.—A large set of buildings in the Strand, close to Somerset House, consisting of a large school and College. Nearest Railway Station, Temple.

KING'S CROSS, at the corner of EUSTON and GRAY'S INN ROADS. is best known as being the centre of Railway Stations, the terminus of the Great Northern Railway being here. The frontage of this Station is very plain, and contrasts unfavourably with the fine building and hotel which constitute the Midland Railway Terminus close by. The huge span of the arch at St. Pancras Station is worth noting. The Midland Hotel was from the design of Sir Gilbert Scott.

KING'S GATE STREET, HIGH HOLBORN.—So called from at one time having a gate at the end of it for the King's use. In this street Dickens made Mrs. Gamp, with her friend, Mrs. Harris, reside. The street is now pulled down to make room for the new road from the Strand.

KINGSTON, SURREY, **on the right bank.**—Distance from London, 20½ miles by water: 12 miles by rail from Waterloo. Railway Stations, Kingston and Surbiton. Derived its name from the King's Stone upon which seven Saxon Kings, from Edward the Elder to Ethelred (A.D. 900 to 971), were crowned.

KNOCKHOLT BEECHES, KENT.—Noted for their size and situation: 770 feet above sea-level: 20 miles from Charing Cross Station.

"LADY'S MILE" (THE).—The carriage road on the north bank of the Serpentine.

LAMBETH, a large London borough extending from the Thames, opposite Westminster, to Brixton and Norwood, has a population of over 300,000, and sends four Members to Parliament.

LAMBETH PALACE, for six centuries the residence of the Archbishops of Canterbury, has witnessed all the Ecclesiastical changes which have taken place since the 13th Century. The Great Hall and Library can be seen from 10 to 4 or 5 on Mondays, Wednesdays, and Fridays, excepting in September. It is situated close to Lambeth Bridge.

LAMB'S CONDUIT STREET leads from the entrance to the Foundling Hospital into Red Lion Street, High Holborn.—It was named after a Mr. W. Lamb, of the time of Henry VIII., who, at his own expense, drew several springs into a conduit in this street.

LAW COURTS: ROYAL COURTS OF JUSTICE.—The huge building in the Strand, close to where Temple Bar used to stand. The architect was Mr. G. E. Street, and it is looked upon as one of his finest works. It is very interesting to walk into the different Courts (there are public galleries to each) and hear judge and counsel thrashing out some troublesome case of litigation.

LAW SOCIETY OF THE UNITED KINGDOM, 103 to 113, CHANCERY LANE.—The Society acts with the Masters of the Courts as Examiners of Candidates for admission to act as solicitors, etc.; it has a Library of 20,000 volumes, and a Club, etc.

LEADENHALL MARKET is an extensive Poultry Market in LEADENHALL STREET All kinds of live birds, etc., can be purchased here.

LEATHER LANE, in HOLBORN, is largely inhabited by Italian colonists, and is the chosen home of large numbers of organ-grinders. On Saturdays the street is full of coster-mongers' barrows.

LEATHERSELLERS' HALL is situated in ST. HELEN'S PLACE, BISHOPSGATE STREET. It belongs to the Leathersellers' Company, which was incorporated by King Richard II. in 1397.

LEICESTER SQUARE.—Dates from 1635, when the first house was built by Robert Sidney, Earl of Leicester. At No. 47 Sir Joshua Reynolds used to live, and on the opposite side, close to the Alhambra, Hogarth spent some of the best years of his life. John Hunter and Sir Isaac Newton also lived here. The Alhambra was rebuilt and reopened in 1883. The Empire is a new and very handsome music hall. Leicester Square was cleared of rubbish and planted with flower-beds and ornamented with a fountain, seats, etc., at the expense of the late Mr. Albert Grant.

LEWISHAM.—A suburb of London 6 miles from Charing Cross; adjoins Greenwich.

LILLIE BRIDGE, WEST BROMPTON.—For Athletic Sports. Reached by District Railway to West Brompton Station.

LIMEHOUSE is situated on the Middlesex bank of the Thames, near WAPPING.—It contains several Ship and Boat-building Yards, Rope Walks, etc.; here is situated the Strangers' Home for Asiatics, Africans, etc.

LINCOLN'S INN became an Inn of Court about the year 1310, after the death of Henry Lacy, Earl of Lincoln, whence the name of the Society is derived.

LINCOLN'S INN FIELDS.—A Square adjoining Lincoln's Inn; at one time it was an open waste used for military exercises, public executions, etc. It measures the size of the base of one of the large pyramids in Egypt. William, Lord Russell, was beheaded here in 1683. It is now open freely to the public, under the London County County Council, and is well patronised by the inhabitants of the overcrowded streets in the neighbourhood.

LIVERPOOL STREET STATION, near BISHOPSGATE STREET, is the terminus of the Great Eastern Railway.—From here is a good service to the Continent *via* Harwich; to the Hook of Holland and Rotterdam daily, Sundays included, Antwerp every week-day, Hamburg twice weekly, and Denmark three times a week; also the Cathedral route for American passengers, etc., between Liverpool and London. It is called the Cathedral route because, at the same fares charged by the more direct routes, passengers are enabled to visit the Cathedrals of Manchester, Lincoln, Ely, and the University of Cambridge, and, at small additional expense, Peterborough and Norwich. This route is of great interest to Americans travelling from Liverpool to London or the Continent *via* Harwich.

LLOYD'S, located in the Royal Exchange, CORNHILL; an institution for insuring and classifying ships.

LOMBARD STREET extends from the MANSION HOUSE to GRACECHURCH STREET, s principally inhabited by bankers; it takes its name from the Longobards, a rich race of bankers, who settled here in the reign of Edward II. Several of the princely old private bankers have their business homes in this street, such as Barclay & Company, Glyn, Mills & Company, Martin's, etc.

" London is not only the largest city in the world, but its business houses are also of a princely magnitude. Among the most prosperous establishments that have grown up in the West End of London in recent years MESSRS. CHARLES BAKER & Co., LIMITED, stand out conspicuously. This enterprising firm, in the short space of twenty years, have built up one of the largest Clothing and Outfitting Businesses in the world. There is no establshment in London where one will see Tweed, Cheviot, and other suits for Gentlemen and Boys in greater perfection of style and material. MESSRS. BAKER & Co. have made the Boys' and Youths' Clothing Department a speciality, for which they have a great reputation; their charges are exceptionally moderate compared with other West End houses."—**Christian Union.**

" MOTHER OF MANY," in **The Queen** NEWSPAPER, says, respecting Boys' Dress: " CHAS. BAKER & Co. I have found eminently satisfactory for my boys. The clothes are singularly inexpensive."

LONDON AND NORTH WESTERN RAILWAY.—The terminus is situated at EUSTON SQUARE for North and North-West of England, also to Ireland, Scotland, Wales, etc.

LONDON AND SOUTH WESTERN RAILWAY Terminus, WATERLOO BRIDGE ROAD.—Main line to Portsmouth, Southampton, Isle of Wight, Exeter, Plymouth, etc.

LONDON BRIDGE.—Built of granite, from the designs of John Rennie, was completed in 1831, widened 1904, and cost £2,000,000. It connects the City with the Borough and the South of London. The traffic is enormous both for vehicles and pedestrians, and is another of those views of London life which the stranger should see, especially at the busy hours of the day. London Bridge Railway Station (South Eastern and London, Brighton and South Coast Railway termini) contributes largely to this traffic. The view down the Thames from the bridge is interesting. The Tower Bridge shows finely, and during the summer season the starting of the passenger steamers for Margate and Ramsgate, Clacton and Yarmouth, etc., adds to the animation of the scene.

LONDON, BRIGHTON AND SOUTH COAST RAILWAY Terminus is situated at South End of LONDON BRIDGE, for Brighton, Eastbourne, Hastings. Victoria Station, Pimlico, is the West End Station for same line.

LONDON CENTRAL MEAT MARKET, SMITHFIELD.—This building, designed by Sir Horace Jones, covers 3½ acres, and is the great centre for the distribution of meat to the Metropolis. It is a busy sight on Friday morning especially, when carriers from all parts of London are to be seen loading their carts for the different suburbs. In addition there are, also, later buildings, constructed in same style, for Poultry, Pork, Fruit, Vegetables, and Fish, and it is to the credit of the City Corporation and to their architect that so fine a series of Markets has been provided. The Cattle Market is at Islington, and the Foreign Cattle Market at Deptford. It was at Smithfield that Bartholomew's Fair used to be held, and it was here, also, in times of religious persecution, that many martyrs were burnt at the stake.

LONDON, CHATHAM AND DOVER RAILWAY Terminus on HOLBORN VIADUCT; serves Canterbury, Ramsgate, Margate, etc.; the Victoria Station, Pimlico, also works this line. The South-Eastern Railway Company have now joined the London, Chatham and Dover Railway in managing under one head the Railway systems of both.

LONDON COUNTY COUNCIL (THE), SPRING GARDENS.—Formed in 1888, when the duties of the Metropolitan Board of Works were transferred to it. It is elected by the ratepayers of the whole of the Metropolis, and, despite much partizanship and increased expenditure, has done good work to justify its existence. The care of the Parks, which have considerably increased since this body was called into existence, has undoubtedly contributed to their popularity, bands being stationed during the summer season on certain days of the week in most of the Parks under their rule. Larger improvements, such as the drainage of the Metropolis, the Thames embankments, etc., the work of their predecessors, have, with the exception of the Blackwall Tunnel, hardly come to their credit; but the new road from Holborn to the Strand, and also the widening of the Strand, are the objects most prominent at the present moment.

LONDON DOCKS are situated on the left bank of the Thames, between St. Katherine Docks and Shadwell, and cover 100 acres. They can accommodate 400 vessels, and the warehouses and vaults store enormous quantities of foreign and colonial products, and, the latter, wine.

LONDON STONE.—A celebrated ancient block of stone, built into the street wall of St. Swithin's Church, Cannon Street, City; it is considered to be the original Central Mile Stone of London.

LONDON WALL.—A portion of the ancient Wall that surrounded London. Can be seen in the Churchyard of St. Alphage, near Aldermanbury.

LONG ACRE.—A street between St. Martin's Lane and Drury Lane, chiefly occupied by carriage-builders. Oliver Cromwell lived here from 1637 to 1643.

LORD CHAMBERLAIN'S OFFICE is in the Stable Yard, ST. JAMES'S PALACE, and the LORD GREAT CHAMBERLAIN'S OFFICE is situate in the HOUSE OF PARLIAMENT, WESTMINSTER.

LORD MAYOR'S SHOW.—Takes place annually on the 9th November, and proceeds from the Guildhall through the Ward over which the elected Lord Mayor presides as Alderman, and thence through the Strand to the Law Courts, returning by way of the Embankment and Victoria Street to the City.

LORD'S CRICKET GROUND is the property of the Marylebone Cricket Club, and here the matches of the Universities, Eton and Harrow, are played. It is also the County Ground of the Middlesex Club, who play here all their home matches. Nearest Station, St. John's Wood, Metropolitan Railway, changing at Baker Street.

LOST PROPERTY OFFICE is in NEW SCOTLAND YARD, the head-quarters of the Metropolitan Police, on the Embankment.

LOWTHER ARCADE, STRAND.—This popular and well-known centre for toys and presents is now closed.

LUDGATE HILL, at the top of which appears the bold west front of St. Paul's (the scene of the Diamond Jubilee out-door service), is perhaps as well known a thoroughfare as any in London. It derives its name from Lud Gate, one of the ancient gates of the City. Nos. 41 and 43, *exactly opposite Old Bailey*, comprise the City Branch of CHAS. BAKER & CO., LIMITED, the Stores for Clothing, Tailoring, and Outfitting. See Price List at end of book.

LUTON.—A busy town, 31 miles from London, famous for the manufacture of straw hats, etc.; the factories are most interesting.

LYCEUM THEATRE, WELLINGTON STREET, STRAND.—This was one of the best known theatres in London; it was celebrated for the splendid acting of Miss Ellen Terry and Sir Henry Irving, and the complete manner in which the plays were produced. It is now closed.

LYRIC THEATRE, SHAFTESBURY AVENUE.—A handsome structure, opened in 1888.

MAGNA CHARTA ISLAND a mile and a half from Old Windsor Lock, near the Middlesex bank.—One of the most charming islands on the River Thames, and of historical interest as the scene of the arrangement between King John and his barons, when Magna Charta was signed, which became the foundation of the freedom of England. It is only fair to say that, as the tradition assigns to the island the honour of being the scene of the signature, in the Charter itself it is said to have been given at *Runigmede* (? if Runnymede); so it seems to be doubtful whether the finishing stroke was given on the island or at Runnymede on the Surrey bank. It was signed in June, 1215.

MALL (THE), a walk on the north side of St. James's Park, extending from Constitution Hill to Spring Gardens.—It takes its name from the game of Pall Mall being played there in old times.

MANCHESTER SQUARE is on the north side of Oxford Street, and contains Hertford House.

MANSION HOUSE.—The official residence of the Lord Mayor. Is about 150 years old, and is overlooking the wide space surrounded by the Bank of England and the Royal Exchange. The Egyptian Hall is a large room in which the Lord Mayor and Lady Mayoress give their banquets, etc.

MARBLE ARCH.—At the west end of Oxford Street, nearly opposite Edgware Road; formerly stood outside Buckingham Palace. The Central Electric Railway between the Royal Exchange and Shepherd's Bush has a station here.

MARGATE, KENT.—Is a very popular seaside resort for Londoners; distance about 75 miles, and is reached by Rail (S. E. & C. Railway); or, in the summer time, by the many large steamers starting daily from London Bridge and Tilbury, down the Thames (by rail from Fenchurch Street). Facing the north-east, it is one of the most bracing watering-places near London.

MARK LANE.—Near Fenchurch Street Station; is celebrated for its Corn Exchange.

MARLBOROUGH HOUSE, PALL MALL, near St. James's Palace.—The London residence of the Prince and Princess of Wales. Built in 1709 as a residence for the Duke of Marlborough, by Sir Christopher Wren.

MARLOW (GREAT), BUCKINGHAMSHIRE, is situated on left bank of the River Thames, 35 miles by rail from Paddington; by river it is 57 miles from London, and 54 miles from Oxford. It is a very favourite place for fishing, boating, and sketching excursions, etc. Within easy walking distance are Henley, Maidenhead, Wycombe, Cookham, etc.; the Quarry Woods are within ten minutes' walk of Marlow Bridge.

MARRIAGE LICENSES in London are obtained at 1, Dean's Court, Doctors' Commons. Hours, 10 to 4; Saturdays, 10 to 2.

MARYLEBONE.—A large parish. The old church in High Street is built on the site of the church in which Hogarth depicted the Marriage of the Rake in the "Rake's Progress." Charles Wesley, younger brother of John Wesley, was buried here.

MASKELYNE AND COOK'S popular conjuring entertainments are given at the EGYPTIAN HALL, just opposite Burlington Arcade; young people are most interested and delighted with a visit here.

MAYFAIR is a most fashionable place of residence, near PICCADILLY. A fair used to be held here on May 1st and following days, but it was supressed in 1708. Lord Beaconsfield died here, in Curzon Street.

MEMORIAL HALL, FARRINGDON STREET.—Stands partly on the site of the old Fleet Prison. It was erected by Nonconformists in memory of the victims of religious bigotry imprisoned here in the reigns of Queen Mary and Charles I.

MERCERS' HALL belongs to the Mercers' Company; is situated between IRON-MONGER LANE and OLD JEWRY, in Cheapside.

MERCHANT TAYLORS' HALL, in THREADNEEDLE STREET, belongs to the Merchant Taylors, a great Conservative City Company. Many Kings, Princes, and nobles have belonged to this Company.

MERCHANT TAYLORS' SCHOOLS, CHARTERHOUSE SQUARE.—One of the great public schools of London, now educates 500 boys, and is under the care and support of the Ancient Merchant Taylors' Company, the master and members attending there on Speech Day (the Feast of St. Barnabas). Edmund Spenser, author of "The Faerie Queen," and Lord Clive were educated at the Merchant Taylors' Company's Schools.

MERTON, in SURREY.—A village on London and Brighton Line. Lord Nelson resided at Merton Place.

METROPOLITAN FIRE BRIGADE (THE) is under the control of the London County Council, the head-quarters being in Southwark Bridge Road, with stations in every large district in London.

METROPOLITAN RAILWAY (THE) and the Metropolitan District Railway, form a circle of Underground Railways round the inner part of London, touching most of the principal railway termini; King's Cross for the Great Northern and Midland Railways; Gower Street for Euston; Edgware Road for the Great Central; Praed Street or Bishop's Road for the Great Western Railway at Paddington; Victoria for London, Chatham, and South Eastern, and London, Brighton, and South Coast Railways. These railways have branches also to the suburbs.

MEUX'S BREWERY.—One of the most celebrated in London; is situated at the Oxford Street end of Tottenham Court Road.

CHAS. BAKER & CO.'S STORES.—Clothing, Tailoring, and Outfitting.—House of Lords and the Sweating System.—At a most exhaustive inquiry recently held on this subject, one of the few firms spoken well of for paying good wages to their work hands was that of CHAS. BAKER & CO., LIMITED. This Company now have six Depots in London for the sale of their superior manufactures, which, being supplied direct to the public from the Company's own workshops, will be found not only well made and in the most fashionable style, but at least 25 per cent. under usual London prices. The Company also keep a splendid assortment of West of England Cloth, Scotch Cheviots, and Irish Tweeds in their Tailoring Departments. Only first-class cutters being employed, the cut, style, and finish are equal to the best West End garments. *See prices on pink pages at end of Book.*

MIDLAND RAILWAY STATION, St. Pancras, Euston Road.—This line runs through the Midland Counties to Scotland. The Midland Railway Hotel, a fine building, adjoins the Station.

MILDMAY PARK.—A suburb of London, near Stoke Newington Green.

MILLWALL DOCKS are situate on the Isle of Dogs, near the West India Docks can be reached by rail from Fenchurch Street Station.

MINCING LANE, City.—Used largely by wholesale dealers of tea, wine, spices, etc.

MINORIES (THE).—A street between Aldgate and the Tower of London, used to be occupied by gunsmiths, armourers, etc.; it takes its name from an old Abbey that used to be here, called the Minories.

MINT, ROYAL, Little Tower Hill.—Where the coinage for the United Kingdom is produced. Permission to visit the Mint can be obtained from the Deputy Master of the Mint (six persons only) on written application.

MITCHAM.—A village in Surrey, noted for its flower farms of roses, and for lavender.

MONKEY ISLAND.—About half a mile below Bray Lock on the Thames, and owes its name to a number of pictures of monkeys with which the Duke of Marlborough adorned a fishing lodge which he built upon the Island. The house is now converted into an inn, which is used by anglers, oarsmen, and camping parties. The accommodation is primitive and cheap. There is a ferry from the island to the Bucks bank. Nearest railway station, Taplow.

MONUMENT, Fish Street Hill, close to London Bridge.—Was erected to commemorate the Great Fire of London in 1666. Admission, 3d. each, from 9 to 4. Nearest Railway Station, Monument (Met.). The number of steps to get to the top is 345. It was begun in 1671 and completed in 1677, at a cost of £13,700. At one time there was an inscription on the side, which ascribed the great fire to "the treachery and malice of the Popish faction, in order to effecting their horrid plot for the extirpation the Protestant religion and English liberties, and to introduce Popery and slavery"; this inscription was cut away in the reign of James II., but restored in deep characters in the time of William III. To the credit of the City, it was finally again cut out in compliance with a vote of the Corporation during the reign of William IV. It is right to say that there does not seem to have been the least reliable evidence to justify the charges made by the inscription.

MORTLAKE is situated on the right bank of the River Thames, near Hammersmith.— Is chiefly noticeable on account of the Oxford and Cambridge Boat Race, from Putney to Mortlake; this race takes place about a week before Easter each year.

MUDIE'S LIBRARY.—This well-known Circulating Library is situated at the Holborn end of Museum Street, near the British Museum.

MUSEUMS.—The following are the Museums that are most interesting to the general public :—

> Bethnal Green Museum.—Nearest Railway Station, Cambridge Heath. Open free on Mondays, Thursdays, and Saturdays, 10 till 10; on Tuesdays and Fridays, 10 till 4, free; on Wednesdays, admission 6d., 10 till 4.
>
> British Museum, Great Russell Street, Bloomsbury.—Nearest Railway Station, Gower Street. Open week-days, 10 till 6. On Sunday afternoons: From 2 till 4 p.m. in Jan., Feb., Nov. and Dec.; 2 to 5 p.m. in Oct.; 2 to 5.30 p.m. in March and Sept.; 2 to 6 p.m. in April, May, June, July and Aug. Free. The Museum is closed on Good Friday and Christmas Day. Guide-books are sold in the Museum.
>
> Hertford House, Manchester Square.—Open free on Mondays, Wednesdays, Thursdays, and Saturdays, Mondays at 12, other days at 10; Tuesdays and Fridays on payment of 6d. Closes: Jan. at 4, Feb. at 4.30, Mar. at 5, Apr. to Sept. at 6. Oct. at 5, Nov. and Dec. at 4. Sundays, open at 2, Apr. and Oct. till 5, May to Sept. till 6. (See Wallace Collection.)
>
> National Gallery, Trafalgar Square.—Open free on Mondays, Tuesdays, Wednesdays, and Saturdays, Sept. to Jan., 10 till dusk; Feb. and Mar., 10 till 5; Apr. to Aug., 10 till 6. Open to Students Thursdays and Fridays 10 till 5, and to the public from 11 a.m on payment of 6d. Free on Sunday afternoons, from Apr. to Oct., inclusive.

CAUTION.—CHAS. BAKER & CO., the well-known Manufacturers of Gentlemen's and Boys' Real West of England Clothing, desire to intimate that their well-known durable manufactures can only be obtained from one of their six London Depots. *See end of Book.*

MUSEUMS—*continued.*

NATIONAL GALLERY OF BRITISH ART, Millbank.—Open free Monday, Thursday, Friday and Saturday. Open to Students on Tuesday and Wednesday, 10 to 5, and Public on payment of 6*d.* Time open: Jan., 10 to 4: Feb. and March, 10 to dusk; April, May, June, July, Aug. and Sept., 10 to 6; Oct., Nov. and Dec., 10 to dusk. Sundays: From April to Sept., 2 to 6; Sept. to April, 2 till dusk. Closed Christmas Day and Good Friday.

NATURAL HISTORY MUSEUM, South Kensington.—Nearest Railway Station, South Kensington. Open daily free, from 10 to 4 or 6; Sundays from 2 to 4 or 7, according to the season.

UNITED SERVICE INSTITUTION MUSEUM.—Open to the public any week-day from 11 to 4 during the winter months, and 11 to 6 during the summer; admission, 6*d.*

VICTORIA AND ALBERT (late SOUTH KENSINGTON) MUSEUM.—On Mondays, Tuesdays and Saturdays the whole of the Museum is open free from 10 a.m. to 10 p.m. On Wednesdays, Thursdays, and Fridays the Museum is open from 10 a.m. to 4, 5, or 6 p.m., according to the season. On these days, being Students' days, a charge of 6*d.* for admission to the Main Building is made for each person, excepting Ticket Holders; but the Museum Buildings to the West of the Exhibition Road are open free. On Sundays the whole of the Museum (excepting the Libraries) is open free from 2 p.m. till dusk.

There are several other Museums in London devoted to special subjects.

MUSIC HALLS.—The following are some of the most important; but there are many other large Music Halls:—

ALHAMBRA, Leicester Square.—Commences 7.45.
EMPIRE, Leicester Square.—Commences 8.
THE PALACE THEATRE OF VARIETIES, Shaftesbury Avenue.—Commences 8.
LONDON PAVILION, Piccadilly Circus.—Commences 7.45.
CANTERBURY, Westminster Bridge Road.—Commences 7.30.
ROYAL, High Holborn.—Commences 7.30.
OXFORD, Oxford Street.—Commences 7.15.
TIVOLI, 65, etc., Strand.—Commences 7.30

MUSWELL HILL.—A suburb about 6 miles from London, now developed into a town of villa residences. The Alexandra Palace is at Muswell Hill.

NATIONAL ART TRAINING SCHOOLS, SOUTH KENSINGTON.—Are maintained by the State. Pupils of both sexes are here trained to become teachers for very moderate fees. Evening classes are held. There is also an evening artisan class held.

NATIONAL GALLERY (THE), TRAFALGAR SQUARE.—The National Collection of Pictures is situated on the northern side of the Square. Open free on Monday, Wednesday and Saturday; Sept. to Jan., 10 to dusk; Feb. and March, 10 to 5; April to Aug., 10 to 6. Open to Students Thursday and Friday 10 to 5, and to the Public from 11 a.m. on payment of 6*d.* Free on Sunday afternoon from April to October, inclusive. The front view of the building is not considered worthy of its position or of the large collection of pictures within. The number of paintings exceeds 1,400, some by gift and others purchased by the nation. One picture by Raphael was purchased from the late Duke of Marlborough for £70,000. The Italian Schools occupy a large proportion of the building, while the Dutch, Spanish, French, and German Schools are all represented. The Old British School includes the paintings bequeathed to it by J. M. W. Turner in 1856.

NATIONAL PORTRAIT GALLERY (THE) adjoins the National Gallery, the entrance facing St. Martin's Lane. The building has three floors, the top one having the portraits of the Tudor, Stuart, and Commonwealth periods, and are very interesting. The other floors come down to the present time, and include those of Queen Victoria and Prince Albert. Admission same hours and days as the National Gallery.

NATIONAL GALLERY OF BRITISH ART (THE) or **TATE GALLERY** was given to the nation by Sir Henry Tate, and is built on a part of the site of Millbank prison—Grosvenor Road, Pimlico, close to Vauxhall Bridge. Nearest Stations, St. James's Park and Victoria. The munificent donor of the building also gave 60 pictures of Modern British Art. In addition to these pictures, the paintings purchased under the Chantrey Bequest and others from the National Gallery, also those of his own works presented by Mr. G. F. Watts. Open free Monday, Thursday, Friday and Saturday. Open to Students Tuesday and Wednesday from 10 to 5, and Public on payment of 6*d.* Time open: Jan., 10 to 4; Feb. and March, 10 to dusk; April, May, June, July, Aug. and Sept., 10 to 6; Oct., Nov. and Dec., 10 to dusk. Sundays: From April to Sept., 2 to 6; Sept. to April, 2 till dusk. Closed Christmas Day and Good Friday.

NATIONAL SCHOOL FOR COOKERY, EXHIBITION ROAD, SOUTH KENSINGTON.—
For teaching the economical preparation of articles of food. Moderate fees.

NATURAL HISTORY MUSEUM (THE), CROMWELL ROAD, SOUTH KEN-
SINGTON.—Contains the Natural History Collections of the British Museum. Is a handsome
building, built on part of the site of the Great Exhibition of 1862. It is 675 feet in length,
and has two towers 192 feet high. The Great Hall is 170 feet long. The departments are
Botanical, Mineralogical, Zoological, Geological, and Ornithological. The latter, showing
t e nesting habits of British birds, is particularly interesting. Open daily, free, at 10 a.m.;
Jᵃn. till 4 p.m.; Feb., 4.30 p.m.; March, 5.30 p.m.; April to Aug., 6 p.m.; Sept., 5.30 p.m.;
Oᶜt., 5 p.m.; Nov. and Dec., 4 p.m. Open Sundays: Jan., Nov. and Dec., 2 to 4 p.m.; Feb.,
4.30 p.m.; March, 5.30 p.m.; May to Aug., 2.30 to 7 p.m.

NELL GWYNNE was buried in ST. MARTIN'S CHURCH, TRAFALGAR SQUARE. She
acted at Drury Lane Theatre in 1666; she lived at 79, Pall Mall from 1670, and died here in
1687. It is said that it was under her influence that Charles II. founded Chelsea Hospital for
old soldiers.

NELSON'S COLUMN is in Trafalgar Square; was erected in 1843 at a cost of
£45,000, and is 145 feet high. The statue of Nelson on top is 17 feet high. The pedestal is
adorned with bronze reliefs and four great lions, the latter modelled by Sir Edwin Landseer.
It commemorates especially the great victory of Trafalgar by which the French Navy was
destroyed and the invasion of England frustrated.

NEW BOND STREET and old Bond Street form one long street containing the
most fashionable shops for costly fancy and other articles in London. Extends from Piccadilly to Oxford Street. Lord Nelson lived at No. 141 in 1797.

NEW CUT.—A street leading out of the Waterloo Bridge Road. It is a market for the
very poorest classes in this neighbourhood: many shops open on Sunday morning.

NEWGATE.—The notorious prison was situated at the corner of Old Bailey and
Newgate Street. It has now been demolished, and a New Central Criminal Court and Session
House are in course of erection. Many infamous criminals have been imprisoned in Old
Newgate, and have there paid the penalty of their crimes. The executions were public until
the year 1868. Readers of "Barnaby Rudge" will remember the wonderful description of the
old prison by Charles Dickens.

NEWINGTON, SURREY.—Extends from St. George's, Southwark, to Camberwell. In
Newington Butts stood Mr. Spurgeon's Tabernacle, which was burnt down in 1898, and is now
rebuilt.

NEW OXFORD STREET.—A short, comparatively new street connecting Oxford
Street with High Holborn. Messrs. Holloway, the proprietors of the well-known pills and
ointment, have their offices here at No. 78, and the proprietors of Pears' Soap have recently
erected magnificent new premises at Nos. 71, 73, and 75, for their offices, which, as a work of
art, are worth inspecting.

NEW RIVER (THE) was constructed to supply London with water; was opened in
1613; it belongs to the New River Company. An original Adventurer's share is worth more
than one hundred thousand pounds.

NORBITON.—A suburb of Kingston-on-Thames, is near Wimbledon Common and
Richmond Park. The walks about Norbiton are numerous, and the scenery is very pretty.
The Royal Cambridge Asylum for Soldiers' Widow's is here; each widow has a furnished
room and 7s. weekly.

NORTHUMBERLAND AVENUE.—A splendid short new street leading from
Charing Cross, containing the Constitutional Club, Grand Hôtel, Hotel Métropole, Avenue
Theatre; close by is the National Liberal Club.

NORWOOD.—A suburb on the London and Brighton Line. Donglas Jerrold was buried in the large cemetery here.

OAKS RACE (THE), run on Epsom Downs in about the last week in May in each year; also the Derby.

OBELISK (THE) at the south end of BLACKFRIARS ROAD stands in the centre of five roads, was erected in 1771 in honour of Bass Crosby, Lord Mayor of London, on account of his obtaining the release from prison of a newspaper printer, who was imprisoned for printing the debates in Parliament, since when they have been fully printed.

OBSERVATORY, ROYAL (THE), GREENWICH.—Founded in 1675. English astronomers make their calculations from the meridian here. The correct time (Greenwich mean time) is settled here daily at 10 o'clock. Greenwich Hospital and Park are well worth seeing.

OLD BAILEY, or Central Criminal Court, close to Newgate. Gives the name to the thoroughfare between Newgate Street and Ludgate Hill. *Immediately opposite Old Bailey, at 41 & 43, Ludgate Hill, is the City Branch of Chas. Baker & Co.'s Stores. See Price List at end of Book.*

OLD BOND STREET.—A street of very fashionable shops, etc., leading out of Piccadilly. It runs into New Bond Street, which leads out into Oxford Street.

OLD JEWRY.—A street leading out of CHEAPSIDE. So called from having been in old times the Jews' quarter of the City.

OLYMPIA.—A large building near Addison Road Station, used for equestrian and other entertainments.

OMNIBUSES run to all parts of London and suburbs at very cheap fares, and the number of them passing through Cheapside to the Strand or Holborn to Oxford Circus is very considerable. In fact, a visitor to London can probably get a better idea of the size and traffic of the Metropolis from the top of an omnibus than in any other way.

OPERA.—The Royal Italian Opera House is situated in Bow Street (Covent Garden Theatre). It is open during the London season.

ORATORY (BROMPTON) (Roman Catholic).—The interior is much admired: in the Lady Chapel is an altar inlaid with precious stones worth £12,000.

ORMOND STREET (GREAT) extends from QUEEN SQUARE to LAMB'S CONDUIT STREET. Many celebrated people formerly lived in this street. The Hospital for sick children (the mother of children's hospitals) is in this street, and is a most valuable institution and greatly appreciated by the poor.

OVAL (THE), KENNINGTON.—The home of the Surrey County Cricket Club, and where a good many of the big matches of the season are played.

OXFORD STREET.—A splendid long street with good shops, leading from Holborn to Bayswater. Several important streets lead out of it, and in about the middle of it is an open space called Oxford Circus, where it crosses Regent Street, another grand street. Oxford Street contains some very good shops, such as Marshall & Snelgrove's, Peter Robinson's, John Lewis', D. Evans', T. Harries & Co., well-known drapers. Jay's well-known fashionable mourning house is in Oxford Circus, leading into Regent Street.

OXFORD AND CAMBRIDGE BOAT RACE is rowed annually, just before Easter, by chosen eights from the two Universities. Oxford has of late years had a series of successes, broken in 1899 by a win for Cambridge, which they repeated in 1900, failed to do so in 1901, but again succeeded in 1902, 1903 and 1904.

PADDINGTON.—A residential suburb at the West End of London; is also noted as containing the terminus of the Great Western Railway, which is connected with the City by the Underground Railway. The Great Western Hotel adjoins the Station.

PALACE ˙YARD.—New Palace Yard is the space in front of Westminster Hall, and a beautiful view of the architecture of the Houses of Parliament is to be seen here, ending with the Clock Tower. Old Palace Yard is between the Houses of Parliament and Westminster Abbey. There is an Equestrian Statue of Richard Cœur-de-Lion here, and a fine view of that side of the Parliament buildings.

PALL MALL.—Named from a French game of paille-maille having been played here. It is now a street of modern palaces and the centre of club life.

PARK LANE.—A street of fashionable residences, that leads from Piccadilly to the west end of Oxford Street, skirting Hyde Park.

PARKS, PUBLIC (THE), AND OPEN SPACES OF LONDON are very extensive.
The principal are :—

> ST. JAMES'S (93 acres), between Whitehall and Buckingham Palace, owing to its surroundings, is one of the most interesting of the Parks. It is tastefully laid out, and there are a number of comparatively rare aquatic birds that seem quite at home in the ornamental waters.
>
> THE GREEN PARK (59 acres), between Piccadilly and Buckingham Palace. At the south-east corner are Stafford House and Bridgwater House.
>
> HYDE PARK (361 acres). The Park, par excellence, of London, thronged throughout the London season, etc.
>
> KENSINGTON GARDENS (275 acres). A continuance of Hyde Park, originally laid out by William III. as the grounds of his Palace at Kensington, which still stands on the western side of the gardens. In one of the south-east rooms of the Palace Queen Victoria was born, 1819.
>
> In N.W. London is REGENT'S PARK (470 acres). The Broad Walk is very popular, and the flower-beds have a display in the Spring and Summer time scarcely bettered in London. The Zoological Gardens are at the northern end of this Park, and beyond them is Primrose Hill, 205 feet in height and 50 acres in extent.
>
> FINSBURY PARK is a popular open space in the North of London, and farther out WATERLOW PARK on Highgate Hill (the gift of Sir Sidney Waterlow) is very pretty and nicely undulated, PARLIAMENT HILL FIELDS, HAMPSTEAD HEATH, and HIGHGATE WOODS. This does not exhaust by any means the list, as in S. London, SOUTHWARK PARK (63 acres), BROCKWELL PARK at Herne Hill, TOOTING, WANDSWORTH and WIMBLEDON COMMONS furnish splendid breathing places for the people.
>
> The S.W. of London has a beautiful Park at BATTERSEA (198 acres) laid out with trees, shrubs, and flowers, with a sub-tropical garden and ornamental water.
>
> The E. and N.E. Districts have VICTORIA PARK (290 acres) for a pleasure ground, whilst farther out are WANSTEAD FLATS and EPPING FOREST.

PARLIAMENT, HOUSES OF.—See HOUSES OF PARLIAMENT.

PATERNOSTER ROW is a narrow street close to ST. PAUL'S CHURCHYARD, so called from being occupied years ago by makers of paternosters, prayer beads, etc.; after that it was occupied largely by silk mercers and lacemen : it is now chiefly occupied by booksellers.

PEABODY BUILDINGS.—Are large ranges of buildings let at moderate rents to the working classes. The funds were provided by Mr. Peabody, an American gentleman who resided in London, who left half a million of money for the purpose. A statue has been erected to his memory at the north-east end of the Royal Exchange.

PECKHAM.—A populous neighbourhood in Camberwell.

PENTONVILLE.—A district in Clerkenwell.

PEOPLE'S PALACE.—Is situated in the Mile End Road. Foundation stone was laid in June, 1886, by the Princess of Wales. Opened by Queen Victoria in 1887. Concerts are given in the large hall, and there are nearly 3,000 students in the evening classes. Nearest Railway Station, Mile End Road.

PETTICOAT LANE.—Leading from Commercial Street, Whitechapel. Is now called Middlesex Street. It is quite crowded on Sunday mornings, shops open, etc., and is one of the sights of this part of London.

PICCADILLY.—A splendid street, leading from Piccadilly Circus to Hyde Park Corner; it contains not only very good shops for high-priced and fashionable goods, but some grand private residences as well. Burlington House, which contains the Royal Academy of Arts and other Societies, is in Piccadilly, also Burlington Arcade, Devonshire House, the mansion of the Rothschilds, Apsley House, the residence of the Duke of Wellington, etc.

PICTURE GALLERIES—

AGNEW'S NEW ART GALLERY, 39B, Old Bond Street.
ACADEMY (ROYAL), Burlington House. Open May to July, admission 1s.
DULWICH GALLERY, at Dulwich.
FLAXMAN GALLERY, University College. Admission free.
FOUNDLING HOSPITAL. Can be seen on Sundays, after service, and other days.
GUILDHALL GALLERY.
HAMPTON COURT.
NATIONAL GALLERY, Trafalgar Square.
NATIONAL PORTRAIT GALLERY, St. Martin's Place, Trafalgar Square.
NATIONAL GALLERY OF BRITISH ART (Tate Gallery), Grosvenor Road, Pimlico.
NEW GALLERY, 121, Regent Street.
ROYAL INSTITUTE OF PAINTERS, 191, Piccadilly. March to June.
ROYAL NAVAL HOSPITAL, Greenwich.
ROYAL SOCIETY OF BRITISH ARTISTS, 6, Suffolk Street, Pall Mall.
ROYAL SOCIETY OF PAINTERS IN WATER COLOURS, 5A, Pall Mall East.
ST. BARTHOLOMEW'S HOSPITAL, Smithfield.
ST. JAMES'S PALACE.
SOANE MUSEUM, 13, Lincoln's Inn Fields.
SOCIETY OF ARTS, John Street, Adelphi.
SOUTH KENSINGTON.
SOUTH LONDON FINE ART GALLERY, Peckham Road.
TOOTH'S, 5, Haymarket.
WALLACE COLLECTION, Hertford House, Manchester Square.

PIMLICO.—A district between ST. JAMES'S PARK and the THAMES.

PLAGUE OF LONDON (GREAT).—1664 and 1665; is said to have been imported from Holland; 4,000 persons are said to have died in one night, and probably at least 100,000 persons perished of this dire disease in two years.

PLUMSTEAD and Plumstead Marshes are situated near Woolwich.

POETS' CORNER is in the South Transept of WESTMINSTER ABBEY, where many celebrated poets are buried.

POLYTECHNICS AND SIMILAR INSTITUTES IN LONDON, for Technical and other Educational Work, Recreative and Athletic Entertainments, etc. (Particulars can be obtained by writing to the Principals or Secretaries.)

*NORTHAMPTON INSTITUTE, St. John Street Road, Clerkenwell.
*BIRKBECK INSTITUTION, Breams Buildings, Chancery Lane.
*CITY OF LONDON COLLEGE, White Street, Moorfields.
NORTHERN POLYTECHNIC INSTITUTE, Holloway Road.
BATTERSEA POLYTECHNIC, Battersea Park Road, S.W.
SOUTH WEST LONDON POLYTECHNIC, Manresa Road, S.W.
EAST LONDON TECHNICAL COLLEGE, People's Palace, E.
GOLDSMITHS' INSTITUTE, New Cross, S.E.
BOROUGH POLYTECHNIC INSTITUTE, Borough Road, S.E.
WOOLWICH POLYTECHNIC, William Street, Woolwich.
REGENT STREET POLYTECHNIC, W.

To which should be added the Institutions of the YOUNG MEN'S CHRISTIAN ASSOCIATION at EXETER HALL, STRAND, and 186, ALDERSGATE STREET, where the religious and social element is added to the different class training given.

* *The Northampton Institute, the Birkbeck Institution, and the City of London College together form the City Polytechnic.*

POOL (THE).—That part of the Thames that extends from London Bridge to Limehouse.

POPULATION OF LONDON AND SUBURBS is above five millions. *(See pages 15 to 17.)* Its rapid strides can be seen by the following figures:—

In 1682 the population of London was	...	...	...	672,000
„ 1700	„	„	...	...	...	700,000
„ 1800	„	„	...	...	...	900,000
„ 1821	„	„	...	...	...	1,378,947
„ 1881	„	„	...	...	...	3,815,544
„ 1891	„	„	...	...	...	4,211,056
„ 1901	„	„	...	...	...	4,536,541
„ 1891 Greater London	...	...	...	...	5,633,332
„ 1901	„	„	...	...	...	..	6,581,372

PORTMAN SQUARE is situated between OXFORD STREET and BAKER STREET. Was built about 1800.

PORT VICTORIA is situated at the mouth of the Medway opposite Queenborough.

POSTE RESTANTE.—Letters to be called for can be addressed at the General Post Office and at Charing Cross Post Office, for the convenience of strangers in London.

POST OFFICE (THE GENERAL), ST. MARTIN'S-LE-GRAND. Postage was reduced to one penny in 1840, thanks to Sir Rowland Hill. The huge business under the rule of the Post-master-General has necessitated the addition of immense new buildings in Aldersgate Street.

PRIMROSE HILL.—Adjoins Regent's Park, near the Zoological Gardens.

PRINCE OF WALES'S THEATRE, COVENTRY STREET.—Opened in 1884.

PRINCESS'S THEATRE, OXFORD STREET.—Rebuilt and opened in 1880.

PRINTING HOUSE SQUARE.—Is where *The Times* is printed; it is situated in Queen Victoria Street, near Blackfriars Bridge.

PRIVY COUNCIL OFFICE is situated in DOWNING STREET, Whitehall.

PUDDING LANE, EASTCHEAP, Lower Thames Street.—The Great Fire of London commenced here in 1666 in the house of the King's baker. It continued four days, and destroyed more than 13,000 houses and 89 churches.

PURFLEET.—A village on the Thames, near Erith.

PUTNEY.—Is situated on the banks of the Thames, about 4 miles from London. The Oxford and Cambridge Boat Race is rowed from Putney to Mortlake.

PYE CORNER, WEST SMITHFIELD end of GILTSPUR STREET.—The Great Fire of London began in Pudding Lane, near London Bridge, and ended at Pye Corner.

QUEBEC STREET.—Is a street leading out of Oxford Street, near Marble Arch named in honour of the taking of Quebec by General Wolfe.

QUEENHITHE.—Is situated in Upper Thames Street; so called from being the hithe or landing place of Eleanor, Queen of Henry II.

QUEEN'S SQUARE, BLOOMSBURY, was named after Queen Anne. It contains several hospitals, also a statue of Queen Charlotte.

RACES.—Ascot Races are run in June. Derby and Oaks are run on about last day of May. The Oxford and Cambridge Boat Race is rowed on second Saturday before Easter.

RAG FAIR.—Is situated in Rosemary Lane, Wellclose Square, Whitechapel.

RAMSGATE.—A seaside watering-place on the South-east Coast, and being only about two hours' railway ride from London, receives a large share of visitors; there are excellent sands, and the sea bathing and climate are good. It is reached also by steamer from London Bridge in summer time.

RATCLIFF HIGHWAY extends from EAST SMITHFIELD to SHADWELL; it is now called ST. GEORGE STREET. Is much connected with seafaring people, and contains Seamen's Mission Hall, Seamen's Chapel, etc. Jamrach, a dealer in wild animals, has an establishment here t No. 179.

READING, BERKSHIRE; distance from London 74 miles by river, 36 miles by rail from Paddington, from Oxford 37 miles by river. It is situated close to the Thames. Huntley and Palmer have their biscuit manufactory here. It is surrounded by beautiful country.

RECORD OFFICE.—Between Chancery and Fetter Lanes; has a fine **new** frontage in the former. Contains the original old Domesday book, and many valuable national documents.

RED LION STREET, HOLBORN.—Leads out of Holborn, and is continued by Lambs. Conduit Street to the Foundling Hospital, to which there is a Chapel attached. The public are admitted to Divine Service on Sundays at 11 a.m. by contributing a small amount at the doors. The service is one of the most beautiful and interesting in London. *(See* FOUNDLING HOSPITAL.) *Exactly opposite Red Lion Street, in Holborn, is situated the Head Depot of Chas. Baker & Co.'s Outfitting Stores.*

REGALIA OR CROWN JEWELS are kept in the Tower of London. Open to the public free Mondays and Saturdays, other days 6d. Strangers should all visit the Tower, as it is one of the most interesting places in London.

REGATTA, HENLEY.—Takes place about the beginning of July.

REGENT CIRCUS, OFORD STREET.—This is much more generally called Oxford Circus, to distinguish it from Piccadilly Circus; it contains several good shops either in the Circus or adjoining, such as Jay's Mourning House and Peter Robinson's large Drapery House.

REGENT'S CANAL commences at Limehouse, runs north to Victoria Park, then turns to the west and skirts Regent's Park, finally joining the Canal at Paddington.

REGENT'S PARK is about 370 acres in extent; it takes its name from the Prince Regent, afterwards George IV. The Zoological Gardens are situated at the north part of the Park, and in the centre are the Royal Botanical Gardens.

REGENT STREET.—One of the finest streets in London. It extends from Portland Place, Regent's Park, to Waterloo Place, Pall Mall; the shops are very good, but are not so fashionable as the Bond Street shops.

RICHMOND, SURREY.—On the right bank of the Thames; 15½ miles distant from London by river; half-hour's railway journey from Waterloo Station. It used to contain the old Royal Palace of Sheen, where Queen Elizabeth died; the Palace stood on the spot now known as the Green. Close by is Richmond Park, about 8 miles in circumference, containing delightful rides and walks, open free to the public.

ROCHESTER, near CHATHAM.—Contains Norman Castle and Cathedral.

ROEHAMPTON.—Is situated near Putney. Go by rail from Waterloo.

ROMAN BATH.—This old Roman bath is situated in Strand Lane, in the Strand; the water in it was supposed to be derived from the neighbouring well of Holywell Street, famed for cures.

ROMFORD.—A place in Essex, about 12 miles from London.

ROTHERHITHE.—A parish on the right bank of the Thames, near Deptford. The Commercial Docks are situated here. It was near here that the old line of battle-ship, the "Fighting Temeraire," was tugged to her last berth to be broken up, and is the subject of Turner's picture.

ROTHSCHILD'S.—The offices of this celebrated financial firm are at New Court, St. Swithin's Lane, E.C.

ROYAL ACADEMY OF ARTS.—See Academy (Royal).

ROYAL ACADEMY OF MUSIC.—Tenterden Street, Hanover Square.

ROYAL COLLEGE OF MUSIC.—Adjoins the Albert Hall, Kensington.

ROYAL ALBERT HALL, KENSINGTON.—Close to Hyde Park and Albert Memorial.

ROYAL EXCHANGE (THE).—The large building close to the Bank of England, facing Cheapside, was opened by Queen Victoria on the 28th October, 1844, and has a fine portico in the classic style, with a large sculpture at the top representing Commerce. The first Exchange, on the same spot, was opened by Queen Elizabeth in 1571. The interior is a large covered courtyard, with a graceful statue of Queen Victoria in the early years of her reign. The panels of the walls are being filled with paintings showing different historical views connected with Commerce and Liberty by eminent artists. The following are already placed in position:—

"Phœnicians Bartering with the Ancient Britons in Cornwall," by *Lord Leighton.*
"London Receiving its Charter from William the Conqueror," by *Seymour Lucas.*
"Queen Elizabeth Opening Gresham's Exchange in 1571," by *Ernest Crofts.*
"Charles the First demanding the Five Members at Guildhall," by *S. J. Solomon.*
"The Fire of London," by *Stanhope Forbes.*
"Queen Victoria Opening the Present Exchange," by *R. W. Macbeth.*
"The Crown offered to Richard III. at Baynard Castle," by *Sigismund Goetze.*

"William the Conqueror Granting a Charter to the Citizens of London," by *J. Seymour Lucas*.

"Sir Richard Whittington Dispensing his Charities," by *Mrs. Ernest Normand (Henrietta Rae)*.

"King John Sealing Magna Charta," by *Ernest Normand*.

Admission inside the Royal Exchange daily from 9.30 to 1.30, and on Monday, Wednesday and Friday, until 3.30. It is used by merchants to transact business, fix the rate of exchange, etc. The public are admitted freely, except in business hours, *i.e.*, between 3.30 and 4.30 p.m.

ROYALTY THEATRE. DEAN STREET, SOHO.

RUNNIMEDE. Ne r Staines and Egham.—Is supposed to be the meadow where King John signed the Magna Charta; but Charter Island, near, is considered the exact spot by some

RYE HOUSE, the scene of the Rye House Plot, is situated near Broxbourne, and is a favourite holiday resort for Londoners. Rye House Station is on the Great Eastern line of railway.

SADDLERS' HALL, 141, CHEAPSIDE.—Belongs to the Saddlers' Company, one of the oldest, if not the very oldest, of the City Companies. The hall was erected in 1822, and the buildings in front in 1864.

SADLER'S WELLS THEATRE, ISLINGTON.—Notable to old playgoers as being the house where Phelps acted for many years. Now a music-hall.

SAFFRON HILL, between HOLBORN and CLERKENWELL, was formerly part of Ely Gardens, and is named from saffron having been grown there. It is much improved now, but used to be a very low and dangerous neighbourhood, largely inhabited by Italians.

SAILORS' HOME is situated at 16, WELL STREET, and DOCK STREET, LONDON DOCKS, E. Branch House, GRAVESEND.

SALISBURY SQUARE, FLEET STREET, is close to St. Bride's Church.—The Salisbury Hotel is situated here, and the square was formerly the residence of many eminent persons. *Lloyds' News* publishing offices are in this square.

SALTER'S HALL, ST. SWITHIN'S LANE, belongs to the Salters' Company, which dates from 1334.—The present hall was opened in 1827.

SALVATION ARMY.—Headquarters are at 101, Queen Victoria Street, E.C.

SANDOWN PARK.—Celebrated for its races. Near Esher 14 miles from Waterloo Station.

SAVOY (THE), in the STRAND, was a palace on the side of the Thames, built in 1245. The Savoy Chapel stands on part of the site, being erected in 1511. It is attached to the Duchy of Lancaster. Sunday services : 10.15 and 11.30 a.m., and 4.0 and 7.0 p.m.

SAVOY THEATRE is entered from the Strand, being adjacent to the Savoy Hotel. It is noted as being the home, since 1881, of the delightful operatic productions of Gilbert and Sullivan, and it woul be difficult to point out any other theatre which has had a greater success than the Savoy. Even now the reproductions of those old operas, "The Gondoliers," "The Mikado," etc., never cease to attract.

SCHOOL OF ARTS.—Adjoins South Kensington Museum.

SCHOOL OF MINES.—Adjoins South Kensington Museum.

SCIENCE SCHOOLS.—Adjoins the South Kensington Museum; the entrance is in Exhibition Road.

SCOTLAND YARD, WHITEHALL.—Is the headquarters of the Metropolitan Police Force. Articles left in omnibuses or other public conveyances are sent to the Lost Property Office here, and are returned to their owners on payment of a small fee.

SERPENTINE (THE).—An artificial piece of water in Hyde Park, formed in 1733.

SEVEN DIALS, ST. GILES'S.—This locality is celebrated as being the heart of one of the poorest districts in London, but has latterly much improved.

SHADWELL.—On the Thames, near the Thames Tunnel.

SHAFTESBURY AVENUE.—A new thoroughfare, leading from Piccadilly Circus to Oxford Street.

SHAFTESBURY THEATRE, SHAFTESBURY AVENUE.—A fine new theatre, opened in 1888.

SHAFTESBURY TRAINING SHIP is the Industrial School Ship of the London School Board, and is stationed on the Thames at Grays,

ST. PAUL'S CATHEDRAL is one of the great centres of London to which every visitor turns. The summit of the hill on which St. Paul's stands has been occupied in succession by temple, monastery and cathedral. The Roman temple is legendary, but the monastery, dedicated to St. Paul, was erected by one of the Saxon Kings in the Seventh Century, and stood until destroyed by fire in 1086.

A Gothic Cathedral was begun by Maurice, Bishop of London, in 1087, and must have been of great extent. It was not completed until 1315; finally it was swept away by the Great Fire of London in 1666.

The present splendid building was designed by Sir Christopher Wren. The first stone was laid on June 21, 1675; the Dome was completed in 1710, the total cost being computed at about a million sterling. Next to St. Peter's at Rome St. Paul's ranks as the largest Christian Church. From the heights surrounding London the Dome is the most conspicuous object in the view over the City. The length of the Cathedral is 515 ft: of the transept, 250 ft. The width of the western facade is 189 ft. The exterior of the Dome is 145 ft. in diameter; interior, 108 ft.; extreme height to top of Cross from ground, 364 ft.

(From a Photograph by Frith & Son, Reigate).

The addition of a Reredos, some beautiful mosaic work in the Choir, and some further ornamentation of the Dome, by Sir William Richmond, have added greatly to the interior effect. On Special Musical Festivals, during Lent, when noted preachers give addresses at mid-day, and on Sunday evenings, the space under the Dome, huge as it is, is filled with large congregations.

From a national point of view, the fact that it is the burial place of WELLINGTON and NELSON, together with many other famous men, will always make St. Paul's a place of paramount interest to English-speaking people. There are fine monuments to both of the great heroes.

Great artists are buried here, including Sir Thomas Lawrence, Sir Joshua Reynolds, Turner, Sir Edwin Landseer, Lord Leighton, and Sir John Millais.

To many the Whispering Gallery and the view from the top of the Dome will be attractive, and access can be gained for a small fee between the daily services, held at 10 a.m. an1 4 p.m.

The Crypt is also open for inspection at a charge of 6d. each visitor.

SHEERNESS, KENT.—On the right bank at the mouth of the river Thames, about 43 miles from London. Sheerness is a fortified dockyard and garrison town, at the mouth of the Medway.

SHEPHERD'S BUSH.—A suburb adjoining Bayswater.

SHEPPERTON,—A village on the Thames, near Sunbury.

SHOE LANE leads out of Fleet Street to Holborn. Near here is St. Andrew's Workhouse, in the burial-ground of which the celebrated boy poet Chatterton was buried. Here are also the printing offices of *The Standard* and *Evening Standard*, with an imposing frontage in St. Bride Street close by.

SHOOTERS' HILL is situated about 1½ miles from Woolwich Common; it commands an extensive view of Kent.

SHOREDITCH. In the East End of London.—Is a busy place for manufacturing, etc.

SKINNER'S HALL, DOWGATE, belongs to the Skinner's Company, who were incorporated in 1327.

SMITHFIELD lies to the back of Christ's Hospital. In ancient times, being a large open space, it was the scene of amusements, tournaments, executions; it was here that Walworth, Mayor of London, slew Wat Tyler, who was the leader of a rebellion. In Smithfield, during the reign of Queen Mary, several Protestants were burned at the stake; it is thought they were burnt just opposite the entrance to the gate of St. Bartholomew's Priory, The Scottish patriot, William Wallace, was beheaded here. For a long time Smithfield was the only cattle market in London, but that is now held at Copenhagen Fields, and the present Central London Meat Market was erected here. There are two churches here, one called St. Bartholomew the Less, within the precincts of St. Bartholomew's Hospital; the other, St. Bartholomew the Great, was founded in 1102. St. Barthomew's is the oldest and probably the most wealthy in London, the income being about £50,000 per annum; Harvey, Richard Owen, Abernethey, and other celebrated men, have been connected with this Hospital.

SOANE MUSEUM, 13, LINCOLN'S INN FIELDS.—Containing Antique Sculptures, Models of Temples, valuable Architectural Library, and a magnificent Sarcophagus, nine feet in length, cut out of a solid block of alabaster, which once contained the mummy of Sethos, the father of the great conqueror, Rameses II.; also some valuable pictures, including Hogarth's "A Rake's Progress." Open free from 11 to 5 on Tuesdays, Wednesdays, Thursdays, and Saturdays, from April to August.

SOCIETY OF ARTS, JOHN STREET, ADELPHI.—Founded in 1754 for the encouragement of Arts, etc. Nearest Railway Station, Charing Cross.

SOCIETY OF BRITISH ARTISTS. SUFFOLK STREET, PALL MALL EAST.—Founded in 1822. Nearest Railway Station, Charing Cross.

SOHO SQUARE is situated on the south side of OXFORD STREET: was a fashionable place of private residence 50 years ago, now is practically devoted to business. It is said to be named from an old cry in hunting the hare.

SOMERSET HOUSE, STRAND.—This fine building, with a frontage to the embankment of 780 feet in length, rising on a terrace 50 feet high, adds to the now imposing range of buildings which borders the Thames between Westminster and Blackfriars. Has also a western wing in Wellington Street, with a principal entrance in the Strand. In the centre of the quadrangle is a large bronze statue of George the Third. The central Inland Revenue offices are at Somerset House; also the collection of wills and registers of births, marriages, and deaths, which may be searched on payment of a small fee.

SOMERS TOWN.—A district near St. Pancras terminus.

SOUTH EASTERN RAILWAY (THE) has a terminus at London Bridge, Cannon Street, and Charing Cross. It runs to Canterbury, Ramsgate, Folkestone, Dover, etc., now being united in one management with the London, Chatham and Dover Company, whose central stations are at Holborn Viaduct, St. Paul's and Victoria.

SOUTHEND.—A lively watering-place on the Essex Coast, 36 miles from Fenchurch St., largely visited in the summer season by Londoners, principally from the East End. It is a very healthy place. The tide recedes a long way at low water. The pier is about a mile and a quarter long, and the large passenger steamers call here on the way to Margate and Boulogne in the season. There are many pleasant excursions from here, and good walks and drives in the vicinity.

SOUTHGATE (OLD).—A village about 8 miles from London. The neighbourhood of Colney Hatch Asylum, which is a growing suburb, 6½ miles from King's Cross, is called NEW SOUTHGATE.

SOUTH KENSINGTON.—A fashionable neighbourhood extending from BROMPTON ROAD to KENSINGTON GORE. The South Kensington Museum and other important institutions are situated here.

SOUTH KENSINGTON MUSEUM, now called the VICTORIA and
ALBERT.—Stands on 12 acres of ground acquired by the Government at a cost of £60,000, purchased by the Commissioners of the Exhibition of 1851 out of the surplus proceeds of that undertaking. This Museum and its surroundings may be justly called the centre of the world of education. After many years the new frontage is being built which will complete the series of Museums, etc., of which this neighbourhood is the centre. (*See illustrations on pages* 50 & 51.) Open free on Monday, Tuesday, and Saturday, and on payment of sixpence on Wednesday, Thursday, and Friday. Hours on Monday, Tuesday, and Saturday, from 10 to 10; Wednesday, Thursday, and Friday, from 10 to 4. Nearest Railway Station, South Kensington.

SOUTHWARK, better known as "The Borough," is on the Surrey side of the Thames, especially the part which London Bridge joins. It is a great centre for the Hop trade, and has also a Borough Market. St. Saviour's Collegiate Church is here, and has lately had a new nave added to its ancient choir and Lady Chapel (built in 1207). Trams from the Southwark side of London Bridge run to the outer suburbs, Brixton, Clapham, Balham and Peckham, at very cheap fares.

SOUTHWARK BRIDGE.—A handsome bridge crossing the Thames between London and Blackfriars Bridges, now free from toll, relieves the heavy traffic of the other bridges. Was constructed in 1815.

SPANIARDS. A well-known inn just across Hampstead Heath, on the road to Highgate.—Has Tea Gardens, etc.

SPITALFIELDS. Near Bishopgate Without.—Is a district noted for silk-weavers. Many French Huguenots, driven out of France by the Edict of Nantes, 1685, lived in this quarter and founded the silk industry here.

SPRING GARDENS is situated between ST. JAMES'S PARK and CHARING CROSS, and was in old times a pleasure garden attached to the King's Palace at Whitehall; the houses built there are now used principally as public offices. The London County Council has its offices here.

SPURGEON'S TABERNACLE.—Situated near the Elephant and Castle; was burnt down in 1898, and is now rebuilt.

STAINES.—A town 19 miles from Waterloo Station, on the Thames; in connection with Egham by bridge. It was near here that King John signed the Magna Charta.

STANDARD THEATRE. SHOREDITCH. A large East End Theatre. Nearest Railway Station, Bishopsgate Street.

STANMORE. MIDDLESEX. Is situated near Edgware and Harrow.

ST. SWITHIN'S LANE. Near Cannon Street Station.—St. Swithin's Church, near, contains the celebrated London Milestone, built in the wall; this was the central milestone, from which all distances were measured; it was originally fixed a short distance away. St. Swithin's Lane contains the Salter's Hall, also the counting-house of Baron Rothschild.

STOCK EXCHANGE (THE). Capel Court, City, is a place more heard of than seen by the general public, as only Members, either Stockbrokers or Jobbers, are admitted. It is the home of speculation, and of wild speculation at times, but it is also, in one sense, the pulse of the nation as representing the value of its interests at home or abroad in the light of current events. The long lists of Government and Municipal Stocks, Railways, Mining and Industrial enterprises daily quoted in the leading papers show what an enormous influence the Stock Exchange wields.

STOKE NEWINGTON —A suburb of London. It has a common of about 5 acres in extent. Abney Park Cemetery here has a monument to Dr. Isaac Watts.

STOKE POGIS.—A village 2 miles from Slough, near Windsor. The old churchyard there was the scene of Gray's "Elegy." The famous Burnham Beeches are near here.

See CHAS. BAKER & CO.'S Price List for Gentlemen's and Boys' Tailoring, Clothing, and Outfitting at end of Book.

STONE OF SCONE is a celebrated piece of stone on which the Scottish Kings used to be crowned, and is now contained in one of the Coronation Chairs at Westminster Abbey; it is of reddish sandstone, and is said to be Jacob's pillow. Old Scottish tradition says that wherever this stone is there will be supreme power of Government.

STRAND (THE).—The famous thoroughfare from the City to Westminster must have seen in pageant or procession nearly everyone who has helped to make history for Britain. Its position has always rendered it one of the most important of London streets. The enormous traffic increasing day by day with the expansion of London has necessitated great improvements in the area near the Law Courts. A new wide avenue, to be called the Kingsway, is being driven northwards to Holborn. Many imposing buildings are to be found in or near the Strand—such as the Law Courts, Somerset House, King's College, Savoy Hotel, and the Hotel Cecil; and several Theatres are to be found on either side of its course, notably The Gaiety, Savoy, Strand, Adelphi, Vaudeville, Terry's, etc.

STRAND THEATRE is situated on the south side of the Strand, near SURREY STREET. Usually devoted to burlesque plays, etc.

STRATFORD-LE-BOW, OR BOW.—A suburb of London, on the Great Essex Road. Bow china used to be made here.

STRAWBERRY HILL.—Is situated between Teddington and Twickenham; is celebrated as containing Horace Walpole's villa.

STREATHAM.—A pleasant and genteel suburb of London. Streatham Common is near it. Can be easily reached by frequent trains from Victoria or London Bridge Stations.

SUB-TROPICAL GARDEN.—Is situated in Battersea Park.

SUNBURY.—A village about 2 miles above Hampton Court; a resort for anglers.

SUNDAY IN LONDON offers a wonderful contrast to the rush of life and business on the other days of the week. The City is deserted and all shops and offices are closed. *See Churches and Chapels for principal places of Worship and t mes of Services.*

SURBITON.—A suburb of Kingston; has grown of late years. Some of the best houses face the River Thames, and it contains villa residences of every size and almost all rents. It is the headquarters of the Kingston Rowing Club and Thames Sailing Club. Stations: Surbiton and Kingston.

SURGEONS (ROYAL COLLEGE OF) is situated on the south side of LINCOLN'S INN FIELDS. The Museum can only be seen by introduction of members.

SURREY AND COMMERCIAL DOCKS are situated at ROTHERHITHE; are largely used by timber-ships. On the north bank of the river at Limehouse, opposite the Commercial Docks, is the entrance to the Regent's Canal, which runs north to Victoria Park and unites with the Paddington Canal.

SURREY THEATRE.—A large building at the south end of BLACKFRIARS ROAD.—The present building was rebuilt and opened in 1865. Noted for melodrama and pantomime.

SUTTON, in SURREY, is about 12 miles from London, on the road to Epsom. The "Cock" is a celebrated house of call on the way to Epsom Races.

SYDENHAM.—Where the Crystal Palace is situated; is about 9 miles from London.

SYNAGOGUES.—The Central one is at 129, GREAT PORTLAND STREET; there are more than sixty in London.

TABARD (THE) was the name of a celebrated inn in Southwark mentioned by Chaucer in the "Canterbury Pilgrims." It was built in the fourteenth century, and burnt down in 1676. It was situated on the east side of High Street, Southwark, opposite St. Margaret's Church.

TALLOW CHANDLERS' HALL belongs to the City Company of that name; it is situated at No. 5, west side of DOWGATE HILL. It was rebuilt in 1871.

TAPLOW, BUCKINGHAMSHIRE, really forms part of Maidenhead, on the Thames.

TATTERSALL'S.—The celebrated horse auction yard is now situated at Knightsbridge. It used to be near St. George's Hospital, Grosvenor Place.

THE TOWER OF LONDON.

THE TOWER OF LONDON is situated on the banks of the Thames, near London Bridge. It was long used as a state prison. It was also a Royal Palace; but is now a Government arsenal, and contains the Crown jewels, interesting collection of old armour, and other curiosities. Open daily, 10 to 4; Mondays and Saturdays free, other days, 6d.

TECHNICAL COLLEGES.—The central institution of the City of London Institute for Technical Education is close to the South Kensington Museum in Exhibition Road, also at Leonard Street, City Road, E.C.

TEDDINGTON, MIDDLESEX.—On the left bank of the River Thames, 18½ miles by river from London, a station on the South-Western Railway, 13½ miles from Waterloo. It is near Bushey Park.

TEMPLE (THE) is situated between Fleet Street and the Thames.—Part of it was built in 1184. It was the quarters of the Knights Templars, a religious order founded in the 12th century to protect the Holy Sepulchre in Jerusalem. The order was dissolved in 1313, and in 1346 the Temple was leased to the students of common law, and ever since it has been one of the centres of legal learning and study in England; the law of England "broadening slowly down from precedent to precedent." It is constituted the Inner and Middle Temples, the Inner being within the City bounds, and the latter being between that and the Outer Temple. The Temple Gardens, running down to the Thames Embankment, are sometimes open to the public, and in early summer-time the Flower Show of the Royal Horticultural Society, the finest show of the kind in London, is held here. It is said that in these gardens were plucked the red and white roses which became the badges of the houses of York and Lancaster. The Middle Temple Hall was built in 1572, and is used as a dining-room; it has a fine oak ceiling and some valuable portraits, one of Charles I. The Inner Temple Hall is also a fine modern building. Libraries are attached to each division of the Temple. The Temple Church, in the Inner Temple, jointly belongs to each of them.

TEMPLE BAR was a gateway that lately stood opposite Child's Bank, between Fleet Street and the Strand. It was removed in 1878 and rebuilt at Cheshunt, in Theobald's Park, the residence of Sir H. Meux. The place where it stood is marked by a monument, which includes statues of Queen Victoria, and King Edward VII., then Prince of Wales, the whole surmounted by the City Dragon, usually termed the Griffin. The heads of persons executed for high treason were formerly fixed on iron spikes over Temple Bar. Temple Bar is the limit of the City Corporation's authority, and on state occasions, such as the Diamond Jubilee, it is the privilege of the Lord Mayor to ride out to meet the Sovereign—which Sir Faudel Phillips did at the Diamond Jubilee of Queen Victoria.

TEMPLE (THE) **CHURCH,** in the Temple, was the old Knights Templars Church; it is divided into two parts—the Round Church, in which are recumbent statues of the old Crusaders, dating back to the 12th and 13th Centuries, and the Choir, in which the musical services are rendered very beautifully. The services are for Members of the Temple and their friends.

TERRY'S THEATRE, STRAND, was built in 1887.

THAMES (THE RIVER) rises at Thames Head, near Cirencester, and runs about 200 miles before it reaches the sea. The most interesting part of it, for Londoners, commences at Oxford, on which the Undergraduates of that University have their practice, hold their races, and prepare their crew for the great inter-University boat-race between Putney and Mortlake every spring. The river runs from Oxford to Abingdon on to Wallingford, Goring, Pangbourne, Reading, Henley, Great Marlow, Cookham, Maidenhead, and Windsor. All these places are delightful river resorts, and attract huge numbers of boating men and parties during the summer. The regattas during the season are largely patronised, especially Henley, which is regarded as the red-letter day or days of the boating season. Hotels on this part of the river are numerous, and a few days' holiday spent here is delightful. Nearer London the river, too, is very pleasant, from Windsor to Staines, Kingston, Molesey, Hampton Wick down to Richmond. There are 32 locks from Oxford to London, and the distance by river is 93 miles. River steamers run from London to Hampton Court during the summer season leaving London Bridge about 9.30 at a cheap fare, passing Chelsea, Putney, Barnes, Mortlake, Richmond and Kew.

Below the Bridges is the Pool, generally crowded with shipping, and on the left are the Custom House, and the ancient Tower of London. In succession follow Wapping with the huge docks, then Limehouse reach, the West India and Millwall Docks, the Isle of Dogs, Blackwall, Greenwich with its Hospital, Naval College, and Observatory, Woolwich with the huge Arsenal, Erith, Gravesend, Tilbury and Sheerness, until the sea is reached at the Nore.

THAMES DITTON, SURREY, on the right bank of the Thames, from London 22½ miles by river, and 89 miles from Oxford; it is opposite Hampton Court Park. Very popular with punt anglers.

THAMES EMBANKMENT.—Magnificent public promenade, between Blackfriars Bridge and Chelsea on the north, and Vauxhall and Westminster Bridge on the South, of the Thames.

THAMES SAILING CLUB, SURBITON, was started to encourage the sailing of small boats on the Thames. Election is by committee: entrance fee, £1 1s.; subscription, £2 2s.

THAMES SUBWAY.—Leads from Tower Hill to Tooley Street, under the Thames.

THAMES TUNNEL.—The work of Brunel, was carried under the River Thames, from Wapping (left bank) to Rotherhithe (right bank), and cost about half a million of money. Is now used for train service by the East London Railway Company.

THAVIES' INN.—One of the old Inns of Chancery, on the south side of Holborn.

THEATRES.—The following are the principal Theatres in London;

ADELPHI, 411, Strand.	IMPERIAL, Tothill Street, S.W.
APOLLO, Shaftesbury Avenue.	LYRIC, Shaftesbury Avenue.
AVENUE, Northumberland Avenue.	New Theatre, St. Martin's Lane.
COMEDY, Panton St., Haymarket.	PRINCESS'S, Oxford Street.
COURT, Sloane Square.	PRINCE OF WALES'S, Coventry Street.
COVENT GARDEN, Bow Street.	ROYALTY, Dean Street, Soho.
CRITERION, Piccadilly.	ST. JAMES'S, King Street, St. James's.
DALY'S, 2 to 8, Cranbourne St., W.C.	SAVOY, Back of the Strand.
DRURY LANE, Catherine St., W.C.	SHAFTESBURY, Shaftesbury Avenue.
DUKE OF YORK'S, St. Martin's Lane, W.C.	STRAND, Strand.
GAIETY, Strand.	SURREY, Blackfriars Road.
GARRICK, Charing Cross Road.	TERRY'S, 105, Strand.
GRAND, High Street, Islington, N.	VAUDEVILLE, 404, Strand.
HAYMARKET, Haymarket.	WYNDHAM'S, Charing Cross Road.
HIS MAJESTY'S, Haymarket.	

The following are some of the many New Suburban Theatres which have lately sprung up all over London :—

ALEXANDRA, Dalston,	MARLBOROUGH, Holloway Road, N.
BRIXTON, Brixton Oval.	METROPOLE, Camberwell.
CAMDEN, High Street, Camden Town.	PRINCESS OF WALES'S, Kennington.
CORONET, Notting Hill Gate.	QUEEN'S OPERA HOUSE, Crouch End.
GRAND, Fulham.	SHAKESPEARE, near Clapham Junction.

Also at Croydon, Lewisham, Balham, Richmond, etc., etc.

THEOBALD'S ROAD.—New Street leading from Holborn towards East End of London.

THREADNEEDLE STREET.—So called from the three needles in the arms of the Needlenaker's Company, is near the Mansion House. Here is located the Bank of England.

TILBURY FORT. In ESSEX, opposite Gravesend. In Charles II.'s time it is said that the Dutch men-of-war came up the river as far as Tilbury Fort. There is a room in the old gateway once occupied by Queen Elizabeth.

TOOTING.—A suburb, near Balham, on the London and Brighton Railway, with a large common.

TOTTENHAM.—Near Stoke Newington. A largely populated suburb.

TOTTENHAM COURT ROAD.—A handsome, broad street leading from OXFORD STREET to EUSTON ROAD. A celebrated public.house, with tea gardens, used to stand at the Euston Road end, and it was the scene in front of this house that Hogarth painted in his celebrated picture, "The Guard's March to Finchley"; this picture is now in the Foundling Hospital, and can be seen, with other valuable pictures, by the public any Sunday after service at the Foundling Chapel. Meux's well-known Brewery, famous for its porter-vats and artesian well, is situated at the Oxford Street end. At the Euston Road end Charles Baker & Co., Limited, have a Branch Depot for their Real West of England Clothing, and although only a branch of this well-known firm, is one of the largest concerns of the kind in London, Next to them come Maple's Furniture Establishment, which stands on several acres of ground, and next is the gigantic Drapery concern of Shoolbred's, who now, in addition to Drapery supply groceries and provisions wines, spirits, etc.

TOURIST'S AGENCIES.—The best known are Messrs. Cook & Son—head office, Ludgate Circus(also at 99, Gracechurch Street, 33, Piccadilly, 82, Oxford Street, etc.); and Dr. H. S. Lunn, 5, Endsleigh Gardens, etc.

THE TOWER.—No other building in England exceeds in historical interest the Tower of London. Said to have had a Roman origin. The authentic builder of the White Tower was William the Conqueror. It was afterwards surrounded by walls and a moat; the present fortifications being constructed by Henry III. It has been a fortress, a Royal residence, and a State prison. It was in the White Tower the abdication of Richard II. in favour of Henry IV. took place, which led to a bitter rebellion. Under a staircase of this tower were found the bones of the two sons of Edward IV., who were murdered by order of Richard III., and are buried in Westminster Abbey. During the 15th Century, when the Civil Wars of the Roses were proceeding, the Tower was the State prison for those who, in turns, became the victims of defeat. During the great religious ferment of the 16th Century the fire of persecution blazed brightly, and amongst the inhabitants of the Tower were Sir Thomas More and Bishop Fisher, two Queens of Henry VIII., Anne Boleyn and Katherine Howard (both executed there), Lady Jane Grey and her husband (the victims of Queen Mary), Cranmer, Sir Walter Raleigh, Duke of Monmouth, Judge Jeffreys, and later, the supporters of the Stuart cause who rose in rebellion in 1745. Thus the Tower becomes to those interested in the far past a great historical fact. In these times it is an historical study. No longer is the Traitor's Gate opened to receive its (unwilling) princely and noble visitors. No longer do the violent differences of claimants to the Throne create the causes which have opened its portals and its dungeons to those who have failed. In the Chapel of St. Peter-ad-Vincula are buried many of these victims. The site of the scaffold is marked on the grounds outside the Chapel. In the Beauchamp Tower the inscriptions of former prisoners are seen carved upon the walls. The collection of armour in the upper floors of the White Tower includes a series of armour-clad equestrian figures from the 13th to the 17th Centuries. The axe and block, too, are grimly suggestive amongst many other exhibits. [Continued on page 89.

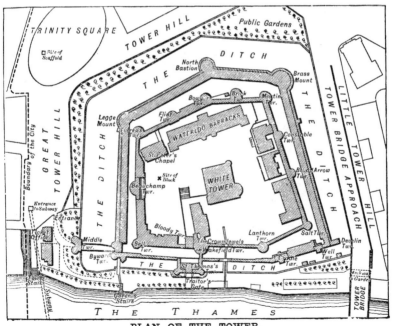

PLAN OF THE TOWER.

THE TOWER—*continued.*

By no means should the Regalia or Crown Jewels be missed. They are exhibited in the Wakefield Tower, and include St. Edward's Crown, used at the coronation of all our kings and queens since Charles II. The different crowns, the royal sceptre, etc., etc., form a collection of great interest.

The Tower is open every day 10 to 4, on Mondays and Saturdays free; other days 1/- each person, 6d. Armouries, 6d. Jewels. Free days between the months of May and September open until 6 p.m. King's Birthday, Prince of Wales Birthday, Easter Tuesday, Whit Tuesday and Coronation day free. The entrance is from Great Tower Hill. The Yeomen of the Guard, popularly known as Beefeaters, have charge of the Tower, and visitors will find the way by their direction to the different points of interest open to the public. All omnibuses to London Bridge from the City pass Eastcheap, an easy distance from the Tower. Mark Lane Metropolitan Station gives the nearest railway communication.

TOWER BRIDGE.—This new bridge crosses the Thames just below the Tower of London and leads into the Minories; it was designed by the late Sir Horace Jones, City Architect, who was the first (in 1871) to conceive the idea of adopting the bascule principle to the centre span in order to admit the passage of vessels, with the two towers in which are placed the lifts and stairs, and which Sir Horace's æsthetic taste enabled him to make salient features in his design. Total length of bridge and abutments 940 feet, width of opening span 200 feet, headway above high water when opened 139 feet 6 inches, headway above high water when shut 29 feet 6 inches, depth of water in opening span at high water 33 feet 6 inches, at low water 13 feet 6 inches.

TOWER HILL stands to the north-west of the TOWER OF LONDON.—Many celebrated people have been beheaded on a scaffold on this hill, among others: Bishop Fisher, 1535; Thomas More, 1535; Earl of Essex, 1543; Earl of Surrey, 1547; Lord Guildford Dudley, 1554; Archbishop Laud, 1645; Earl of Strafford, 1641; and Lord Lovat, 1747, who was the last person beheaded in England.

TOWER SUBWAY.—A curious feat of engineering skill, in the shape of an iron tube 7 feet in diameter, driven through the bed of the Thames between Great Tower Hill (left bank) and Vine Street (right bank).

TRAFALGAR SQUARE, with Nelson's Monument as the centre of attraction, is bordered on the north side by the National Gallery, the architecture of which has received much criticism, the word "pepper-boxes" being given to the three towers of it. St. Martin's Church stands at the corner of the Square. Statues of Napier, Havelock and Gordon are erected in the Square, and two large fountains give a refreshing effect to the whole scene. It is one of the best known open spaces in London.

TREASURY. WHITEHALL, S.W.—Hours, from 11 to 5. Station, Westminster Bridge.

TRINITY HOUSE, TOWER HILL.—The Board has control of the Pilotage, Beaconage, etc., of the United Kingdom. Nearest Railway Station, Cannon Street.

TUSSAUD'S (MADAME).—Wax Works. One of the oldest Exhibitions in London; used to be in Baker Street; is now removed to magnificent new headquarters in the Marylebone Road; close to Baker Street Station. Admission, 1/-; 6d extra for Napoleon Room and Chamber of Horrors.

TWICKENHAM, MIDDLESEX.—On the left bank of the River Thames, 17½ miles from London by river, 11½ by rail from Waterloo. It is a long rambling village, stretching towards Bushey and Teddington; it is practically a suburb of Richmond. The poet Pope died here in 1744.

TYBURN GATE.—The real site of this spot is a matter of dispute. An iron slab opposite the end of Edgware Road, and about 50 yards west of Marble Arch, professes to point out the exact spot; but No. 49, Connaught Square, some 200 or 300 yards north-west of that spot, disputes with it the doubtful honour. Nearest Railway Station, Edgware Road.

UNITED SERVICE INSTITUTION MUSEUM.—The building in which the interesting Museum of this Institution is now housed is the Banqueting Hall of the old Whitehall Palace. It was designed by Inigo Jones and erected during the reign of James I., and is the only portion of the old palace which was saved when the rest of the buildings were destroyed by fire during the reign of James II. The magnificent painted ceiling is one of the masterpieces of the great Flemish painter, Rubens, and is probably unrivalled in the world for its colouring and beautiful execution. The Museum contains the celebrated models of the Battles of Trafalgar and Waterloo, a splendid collection of models of ships from an early period, including models of some of our latest battleships, cruisers, destroyers, etc., together with a fine collection of arms, of all periods, Nelson, and many other Naval and Military relics of historical interest. The Museum is open to the public any week-day from 11 to 4 during the winter months, and 11 to 6 during the summer; admission, 6d. It was outside the Banqueting Hall, at the north-west corner, that the scaffold was erected on which Charles I. was beheaded; he passed through the Hall on his way to execution, and his dead body lay in the Hall until removed for burial.

THE TOWER BRIDGE (open for River Traffic).

THE TOWER BRIDGE, commenced in 1886, completed in 1894.
Architect, the late Sir Horace Jones. Engineer, Mr. John Wolfe Barry. Resident Engineer, Mr. E. W. Cruttwell.
For Foundation and Northern Approach, Mr. John Jackson. For Southern Approach, Mr. William Webster.
Contractors { For Iron and Steel Work of Superstructure, Sir Wm. Arrol & Co., the builders of the Forth Bridge.
For Machinery, Sir William Armstrong, Mitchell & Co., Ld. For Masonry of Towers, Messrs. Perry & Co.
Total length of Bridge and Abutments, 940 feet. Total length of Bridge and approaches, 2,640 feet. Opening span, 200 feet.

UNIVERSITY BOAT RACE.—Is rowed annually between Oxford (Dark Blue) **and** Cambridge (Light Blue), on about the Saturday before Passion Week, between Putney **and** Mortlake. The best points of view are at Chiswick; on Barnes Terrace; or, best of all perhaps, on Barnes Railway Bridge, tickets for which are to be had at Waterloo Railway Station.

UNIVERSITY COLLEGE AND SCHOOL, GOWER STREET.—Has a large number of Scholarships, total value above £2,000 per annum, most of which are open to Lady Students. Nearest Railway Station, Gower Street (Met.).

UNIVERSITY OF LONDON, lately at BURLINGTON GARDENS, PICCADILLY. now taking possession of a large part of the Imperial Institute, South Kensington. Incorporated by Royal Charter in the first year of the late Queen's reign.

UXBRIDGE.—16 miles from London, on Great Western Railway, a Market Town in Middlesex.

VAUDEVILLE THEATRE, 404, STRAND.—Nearest Railway Station, Charing Cross.

VAUXHALL BRIDGE connects VAUXHALL with MILLBANK. Is now being rebuilt, and a temporary bridge opposite the Tate Gallery is used in its place.

VAUXHALL PARK is situated in SOUTH LAMBETH ROAD, size about 7 or 8 acres.

VETERINARY COLLEGE. MUSEUM, GREAT COLLEGE STREET, CAMDEN TOWN.— Admission daily from 9 a.m. to 5 p.m. on presentation of card.

VICTORIA DOCKS.—Near the London Docks, Canning Town.

VICTORIA EMBANKMENT.—Extends along the left bank of the Thames, from Westminster to Blackfriars, and was constructed by Sir Joseph Bazalgette. Cleopatra's Needle, Temple Gardens, good view of the River, Houses of Parliament, are among the attractions.

VICTORIA PARK.—One of the largest and finest in London, 217 acres in extent, lies to the north-east; most crowded on Saturday and Sunday evenings. Nearest Railway Station, Victoria Park (N.L.) and Cambridge Heath (G.E.R.).

VICTORIA RAILWAY STATION is situated at the west end of VICTORIA STREET, WESTMINSTER; is the West End Terminus of the S.E. & C.R. and L.B. & S.C.R.

VICTORIA THEATRE, NEW CUT, LAMBETH.—Stations, Waterloo and Blackfriars.

VINTNER'S HALL, situate at 68, UPPER THAMES STREET, belongs to the Vintner's Company. Rebuilt in 1823.

VINTRY (WARD OF) is situated between CANNON STREET and DOWGATE.

VIRGINIA WATER.—A very pretty piece of ornamental water near Windsor, and well worth a visit. It was formed in 1746 by the Duke of Cumberland, the victor at Culloden, to drain the surrounding land. It can be reached from Waterloo Station. Near here the late Mr. Holloway has erected a sanitorium for the insane, and the Holloway College for the Higher Education of Women, at a cost of a quarter of a million of money.

WALLINGFORD, BERKSHIRE, on the right bank of Thames, 90 miles by water from London. 21 miles from Oxford, is a very ancient town, with remains of Roman fortifications, etc.

WALTHAM ABBEY.—By Great Eastern Railway. The Abbey, powder mills, fishing, etc.

WALTHAMSTOW.—A suburb of London, reached from Liverpool Street Station.

WALTON, SURREY.—On right bank of the Thames, distance by water, 28 miles from London, 83 from Oxford. From St. George's Hill can be obtained a very fine view extending over seven counties.

WALWORTH.—A thickly populated suburb of London on Surrey side of Thames.

WANDSWORTH.—A suburb of London near Battersea.

WANDSWORTH BRIDGE crosses the Thames about a mile below PUTNEY, and connects Wandsworth with the extreme west of London.

WAPPING.—On the Thames, opposite Rotherhithe. The birthplace of Arthur Orton, of Tichborne notoriety; its landing-place is known as "Wapping Old Stairs."

WARDOUR STREET.—Leading out of Oxford St. Is noted for old curiosity shops.

WAR OFFICE. PALL MALL. Hours, 10 a.m. to 5 p.m.

WATER COLOURS (ROYAL INSTITUTE OF PAINTERS IN). 189, PICCADILLY.— Exhibition commences at end of April; admission, 1s. Nearest Railway Station, Charing Cross.

WATER COLOURS (ROYAL SOCIETY OF PAINTERS IN) Gallery, 5A, PALL MALL EAST, S.W.—This Society (often called the Old Society) was founded in 1804, and has held annual Exhibitions since that year. The Summer Exhibition is open to the public towards the end of April, and the Winter Exhibition usually opens in November. Railway Station, Charing Cross.

WATERLOO BRIDGE, one of the finest London bridges, was completed in 1817 at a cost of £1,000,000. A fine view is obtained from it of the Embankment, the Houses of Parliament, etc., also, looking east, of St. Paul's, etc.; it leads to Waterloo Road, out of which is the terminus of the London and South-Western Railway, Waterloo Station.

WATERMEN'S COMPANY is an old guild dating from the fourteenth century, who for many generations had the monopoly of the navigation of the Thames.

THE LAW COURTS (opened by Queen Victoria in 1882) were erected from the designs of the great architect, the late Mr. G. Street, R.A., on the north side of the Strand, just beyond the site of Old Temple Bar. The building has a frontage to the Strand of 500 feet, and extends back to Carey Street, Lincoln's Inn. The Clock Tower is 160 feet high. The Central Hall is 230 feet long. The cost of buildings and land was over £2,000,000.

THE WALLACE COLLECTION,

HERTFORD HOUSE, MANCHESTER SQUARE.

PLAN OF GROUND FLOOR.

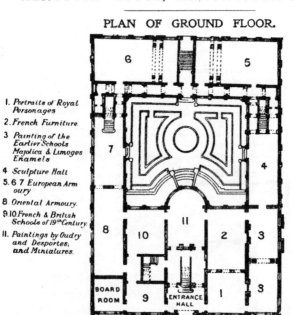

1. *Portraits of Royal Personages*
2. *French Furniture.*
3. *Painting of the Earlier Schools Majolica & Limoges Enamels*
4. *Sculpture Hall*
5. 6 7 *European Armoury*
8. *Oriental Armoury.*
9. 10. *French & British Schools of 19th Century.*
11. *Paintings by Oudry and Desportes, and Miniatures.*

WALLACE COLLECTION (THE), at HERTFORD HOUSE, MANCHESTER SQUAI E, is another of, and the latest addition to, the public Art Galleries of London. This fine collection of Pictures, Miniatures, Bronzes, Armour and Arms, Furniture, Porcelain, and other precious Works of Art was brought together by the third and fourth Marquises of Hertford, and was considerably added to and re-organised by Sir Richard Wallace, to whom it had passed by bequest. It was finally bequeathed to the Nation by the late Lady Wallace in 1897, and was opened in 1900 The pictures include the works of French artists of the 18th century—Watteau, Fragonard, Greuze, etc., who are more largely represented here than in any other public or private gallery in Europe, except the Louvre, and also of the celebrated French artists of the 19th century, many of whom are not represented in any other public gallery in London. Those of Prudhon, Delacroix, Ary Scheffer, Decamps, Vernet, Meissonier (whose small and beautiful paintings are one of the delights of the collection, in Room 15), Delaroche, Gerome, Corot, etc. There are also works of the Italian and Spanish schools, the latter including Velasquez and Murillo. The Flemish school, with pictures by Rubens, Van Dyck, and many others, has fine examples, whilst the Dutch school, with its Rembrandts and famous works of other artists, is slendidly represented. *(Contd.)*

WALLACE COLLECTION—*continued.*

England is represented by some fine portraits by Sir Joshua Reynolds, Gainsborough, and works by Romney, Lawrence, Turner, Wilkie, Stanfield, David Roberts, etc.

The collection of Porcelain, Italian Majolica, French Furniture of all kinds, Clocks, Bronzes, and other ornamental objects of the 17th and 18th centuries is said to be unique, no single collection in France or England being so complete.

The Galleries of Armour and Arms (5, 6, and 7 for European, and 8 for Oriental) display a collection which "was formed chiefly to demonstrate the beauty of the armourer's art of nearly all periods and nationalities."—Guide books of the pictures, 6*d.* ; abridged, 2*d.* ; and of the Armoury, 6*d.*, the latter being necessary for those wishing to know the period and country to which the different arms and armour belong.

THE WALLACE COLLECTION is open to the public free on Mondays from 12 noon, and on Wednesdays, Thursdays, and Saturdays from 10 a.m. until 6 during the summer months, closing earlier during the winter months. Also open on Sundays free during the summer months from 2 till 6. Admission on Tuesdays and Fridays, 11 till 6, 6*d.*

The nearest station by the Central Electric Railway (Twopenny Tube) is Bond Street, the turning nearly opposite Duke Street, leading direct to Manchester Square. All omnibuses through Oxford Street from Oxford Circus to Marble Arch pass this turning.

PLAN OF FIRST FLOOR.

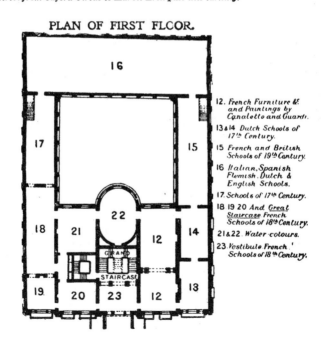

12. *French Furniture &. and Paintings by Canaletto and Guardi.*

13 & 14 *Dutch Schools of 17th Century.*

15 *French and British Schools of 19th Century.*

16 *Italian, Spanish Flemish, Dutch & English Schools.*

17. *Schools of 17th Century.*

18 19 20 And *Great Staircase* French *Schools of 18th Century.*

21 & 22. *Water-colours.*

23 *Vestibule French Schools of 18th Century.*

WATLING STREET. CITY.—Forms part of the old Roman road from Dover **through** London to Chester.

WAX CHANDLER'S HALL is situated in GRESHAM STREET WEST, and belongs to the Wax Chandler's Company.

WAXWORKS (MADAME TUSSAUD'S). This celebrated exhibition is situated in the MARYLEBONE ROAD, near Baker Street Station. It consists of a large collection of wax figures of celebrated persons; in many cases the dresses are the same as actually worn by the persons represented. Admission 1s.

WEAVERS' COMPANY is a very old Livery Company of London. Was incorporated by Henry II. in 1184.

WELSH HARP. HENDON.—A popular place of amusement; has lake for boating, skating, fishing, etc.

WESLEY (JOHN), the founder of Methodism, was buried in the Wesleyan Chapel in the City Road, opposite the entrance to Bunhill Fields.

WEST INDIA DOCKS are situated between LIMEHOUSE and BLACKWALL on the left bank of the Thames. Were opened in 1806.

WESTMINSTER (THE CITY OF) has now, under the new London Municipal Act, once more its Mayor and Corporation. It extends from Kensington to Temple Bar, and, with about 200,000 inhabitants, sends three members to Parliament.

WESTMINSTER ABBEY.—There are few buildings in England—probably excepting the Tower, not one—that can compare with Westminster Abbey in historical interest. Originally built by Edward the Confessor, whose once bejewelled shrine is still at the back of the High Altar, it was rebuilt by Henry III. in the early part of the twelfth century. The main part of the present edifice dates from that period, and is a beautiful specimen of Gothic architecture. The Church is built in the form of a Latin cross ; the architecture of the nave, choir, and transepts being Early English. Henry VII. destroyed the Lady Chapel, erected at the east end by Henry III., and constructed in the latter part of the fifteenth century the very beautiful Chapel (Tudor Gothic) which bears his name, and in which he and his Queen, Elizabeth, lie buried.)

In the Choir, and immediately before the Great Altar, is the spot where the Kings and Queens of England have been crowned since 1066. One can scarcely help being impressed, however elementary their knowledge of history may be, with the fact that it was, at least, on this site, that William the Conqueror, who defeated Harold at Hastings, was made King in 1066; that Willim Rufus, who was killed by an arrow in the New Forest, was also crowned in 1097 ; that Richard the Lion-hearted, in 1089; and each succeeding line of Monarchs (the Plantagenets, the Tudors, the Stuarts, followed by the Hanoverian dynasty) up to the present time. From the time when the Barons went forth from their castles with vassals and retainers to fight with cross-bows and battle-axes, very often amongst themselves, or as Crusaders to the Holy Land, down to the era when greater liberty, comfort and security is enjoyed by the people than has ever before been known in England, the following Kings and Queens have been crowned in Westminster Abbey since it was founded :—

William the Conqueror	Dec. 25, 1066	Henry VII. ...	Oct. 30, 1485
Matilda	May 11, 1068	Elizabeth of York	Nov. 25, 1487
William Rufus	Sept. 26, 1087	Henry VIII.	June 24, 1509
Henry I.	Aug. 5, 1100	Anne Boleyn	June 1, 1533
Matilda	Nov. 11, 1100	Edward VI.	Feb. 20, 1547
Stephen	Dec. 26, 1135	Mary ...	Oct. 1, 1553
Henry II.	Dec. 19, 1154	Elizabeth	Jan. 15, 1559
Richard I.	Sept. 3, 1189	James I.	July 25, 1603
John ...	May 27, 1199	Charles I.	Feb. 2, 1626
Henry III.	May 17, 1220	Charles II.	Apl. 23, 1661
Edward I. and Eleanor	Aug. 19, 1274	James II.	Apl. 23, 1685
Edward II.	Feb. 25, 1308	William and Mary	Apl. 11, 1689
Edward III.	Feb. 1, 1327	Anne...	Apl. 23, 1702
Richard II.	July 16, 1377	George I.	Oct. 20, 1714
Henry IV.	Oct. 13, 1399	George II. and Queen Caroline	Oct. 11, 1727
Henry V.	Apl. 9, 1413	George III. and Queen Charlotte	Sept. 22, 1761
Catherine	Feb. 24, 1421	George IV. ...	July 19, 1821
Henry VI.	Nov. 6, 1429	William IV. and Queen Adelaide	Sept. 8, 1831
Margaret	Apl. 30, 1445	Queen Victoria	June 28, 1838
Edward IV.	June 28, 1461	Edward VII. and Queen Alex-	
Richard III.	July 6, 1483	andra ...	Aug. 9, 1902

Continued on page 96

INTERIOR OF HENRY VII.'S CHAPEL, WESTMINSTER ABBEY.

(By permission of Messrs. Geo. Bell & Son.

WESTMINSTER ABBEY—*continued.*

The services are daily at 10 and 3 o'clock; Sundays at 11, 3, and 7 o'clock. The nave and transepts, including the Poets' Corner, are open in summer until 6 o'clock, but in winter are closed when the afternoon service is ended.

The Chapels and Royal Tombs are open, free, to the public on Mondays and Tuesdays; on other weekdays, admission 6*d.* They are well worth a visit, and include the shrine of Edward the Confessor, the monuments, with recumbent figures, of Henry III., Henry V. and his Queen Katherine, Edward III. and his wife Phillippa, Richard II., Edward I., and Henry VII. and his Queen, in the chapel bearing his name. In the north aisle of this chapel is the monument and burial-place of Queen Elizabeth and her predecessor, Queen Mary; also the remains of the young princes murdered in the Tower. In the South aisle is buried Mary Queen of Scots, and equal honour seems to have been paid to her memory as to Elizabeth, Charles II., William III., and Mary, and Queen Anne.

The Coronation Chair is to be seen in Edward the Confessor's Chapel. The Jerusalem Chamber, the scene of the death of Henry IV., has rich frescoes and old stained glass, and the Chapter House, built in the 13th century, was from then to 1547 used for the meetings of Parliament.

In these later times Westminster Abbey still holds its position as the burial-place of most of the great men who have adorned their country either as statesmen, poets, dramatists, historians, discoverers, etc. If not buried there, some memorial of them is noted. The well-known monument to Shakespeare is an instance in the Poets' Corner, although he is buried at Stratford-on-Avon. Charles Dickens the younger (now deceased) says: "The fact that the sightseer is at every step treading upon the graves of England's wisest and noblest cannot but render a visit to Westminster Abbey a thing to remember."

WESTMINSTER BRIDGE.—A handsome, wide bridge, close to the Houses of Parliament and leads into the Westminster Bridge Road, on the Surrey side of the river. A fine view is to be obtained here of the river frontage of the Houses of Parliament, with St. Thomas's opposite.

WESTMINSTER HALL.—If the Houses of Parliament are a monument of the Victorian period of progress, Westminster Hall is representative of the past, being built by William Rufus and rebuilt in the 13th and 14th Centuries. In this Hall were held the early English Parliaments, and here, down to George IV., the English monarchs held their coronation festivals. Memorable State trials have been held here. Charles I., William Wallace, Sir Thomas Moore, Guy Fawkes, the Earl of Strafford, were all tried and condemned to death in this Hall. Warren Hastings was also tried here and acquitted. The Hall is surrounded by statues of our kings and Queens, and its fine roof is greatly admired.

WESTMINSTER SCHOOL, DEAN'S YARD, THE SANCTUARY, WESTMINSTER, is another of the large public schools, being refounded by Queen Elizabeth in 1560. The dormitory of the Abbey is used as the schoolroom, whilst the dining-room is the old Abbots' Refectory. A Greek comedy is performed here at Christmas by the boys, with prologue and epilogue on public events. Ben Jonson, Cowper, Sir Christopher Wren, George Herbert, Warren Hastings, and J. A. Froude, the historian, were educated here. On the south side of Dean's Yard are the buildings of the Church House, in which the Houses of Convocation meet.

WHITECHAPEL.—A busy thoroughfare in the East End of London.

WHITEFRIARS. At the back of the south side of Fleet Street.—Was the site of a convent of Carmelites, founded 1244.

WHITEHALL. Opposite Horse Guards.—Erected by Inigo Jones. The banqueting-room is the only remaining part of the Royal Palace of Whitehall. King Charles I. was beheaded here. It is probable that the War Office will be moved to new buildings here, immediately opposite the Horse Guards.

WHITEFIELD'S TABERNACLE.—A celebrated dissenting place of worship in Tottenham Court Road, Toplady, the author of "Rock of Ages," lies buried here. A large and handsome building is now erected here.

WHITTINGTON'S ALMSHOUSES.—Are situated on Highgate Hill, near the spot where he is said to have heard Bow Bells telling him to return to London. A stone marks the spot.

See **CHAS. BAKER & CO.'S** Price List for Clothing, etc., at end of Book.

WILL AND PROBATE OFFICE is situated at SOMERSET HOUSE, STRAND; also Registrar's Office of Birth's, Deaths, and Marriages, Inland Revenue, etc.

WIMBLEDON COMMON affords some beautiful walks within easy reach of London.—The National Rifle Association met here annually up to 1889. It adjoins Putney.

WINDSOR CASTLE. The great English palace of our reigning Monarch, is one of those places which everyone, whether visitor or inhabitant of London, should take a journey to. It is within easy distance of the Metropolis, is reached either by Great Western Railway from Paddington, or the South-Western Railway from Waterloo, and is about 21 miles distant. A daily Return Ticket can be obtained from either company for 2s. 6d. The splendid position of the Castle, overlooking the Thames, its massive Round Tower, and bold architectural front, is one of the sights for every Englishman to see. When the Court is absent the State Apartments and all principal portions of the Castle are open to the public on Mondays, Tuesdays, Thursdays, Fridays, and Saturdays, and it is an advantage to select a day for a visit here when the interior can be seen. The view from the Round Tower is very extensive and ranges over many counties, including the Great Park and Eton College close by, which can also be seen from the Terrace.

The suite of State Apartments to which the public are admitted consists of the following rooms :The Van Dyck Room, the Zuccarelli Room, the State Ante-Room, the Grand Vestibule, the Waterloo Chamber, the Grand Reception Room, St. George's Hall, the Guard Chamber, the King's Presence Chamber, and the King's Audience Chamber. Throughout these Apartments are seen a splendid collection of pictures, tapestry, china, and rich furniture.

St. George's Chapel, within the precincts of the Castle, was constructed by Edward IV. (whose tomb is in the North Aisle), and is closely associated with the Order of the Garter. The beautiful Choir, besides being set apart for the services of the Church, is also used for the ceremony of installing the Knights of the Garter. The banners of the different knights hang over each stall, being emblazoned with the different armorial bearings, etc. Over the Altar is the Albert Memorial Window, designed by the late Sir Gilbert Scott. In the Choir Henry VIII., his Queen, Jane Seymour, and Charles I. lie buried. A cenotaph of the Princess Charlotte attracts a large amount of attention in one of the minor Chapels. The Albert Chapel, richly restored by Queen Victoria (who now rests with her husband in the Royal Mausoleum at Frogmore), adjoins the east end of St. George's Chapel.

Windsor Park, the Long Walk of which comes right up to the Castle, and is three miles long, is very beautiful in summer.

WOOD STREET.—Leading from Cheapside to London Wall, is the headquarters of some of the best-known firms in London, such as I. & R. Morley, the great Hosiery Manufacturers; Dent, Allcroft and Co,, Glove Manufacturers; and many others. At the corner of this street stands the tree referred to by Wordsworth in his verses on "Poor Susan."

WOOLWICH ARSENAL.—Here are made the whole of the Ordnance for the Naval and Military Services. Visitors must be furnished with a ticket from the War Office. The Artillery Barracks, the headquarters of the Royal Horse and Foot Artillery, are situated near the Arsenal. Trains run here from Fenchurch Street and Liverpool Street Stations.

WORMWOOD SCRUBBS.—A common near Notting Hill. Has a convict prison erected on part.

WYCH STREET.—An old street leading from the Strand to Drury Lane.

ZOOLOGICAL GARDENS (THE) REGENTS PARK, N.W.—The popularity of these Gardens amongst Londoners is such, that if the whole of the Metropolis were polled, *including the children,* we question very much if any other permanent institution would gain half the number of votes. The lions and the tigers, the seals and sea-lions, the bears (especially the Polar), the giraffes, the elephants, hippopotamuses and rhinoceroses, the camels, the kangaroos, the birds and parrots and parrakeets, only to be exceeded, to the children, by the monkeys, who, in their house, are visited on popular days by a crowd delighted by the antics and gesticulations of its inhabitants. There is a reality about

ZOOLOGICAL GARDENS—*continued.*

a collection of animals from all parts of the world, such as this is, which is a never failing attraction. Whilst we have the prophecy of Mr. Gambier Bolton that during the lifetime of the youngest of this generation many of the wild species of animals will have died out through the pressure of advancing civilisation, let us hope it is a fallacious one, and that "The Zoo" may be an institution of pleasure and instruction "e'en when our babes are old."

It is a pretty sight on a fine summer afternoon to see the elephants, camels, and dromedaries, carrying their living freight of merry children round the Gardens.

Feeding times in summer are at 4 o'clock, and from November to February at 3 o'clock. It is an interesting time for visitors, and particularly so for the animals.

The Gardens are open from 9 o'clock A.M. till sunset daily, admission 1s., children 6d., on Mondays 6d. each. On Sundays admission is only obtained by member's ticket. A pleasant way of reaching the Zoological Gardens is by rail or 'bus to Portland Road Station, thence walking three-quarters of a mile through Regent's Park to the main entrance. The North entrance is half a mile from Chalk Farm, and three-quarters of a mile from St. John's Wood Road (Metropolitan). The "Waterloo" omnibuses from Camberwell Gate, S.E., come up from South London *via* Waterloo Bridge, Strand, Regent Street, to Great Portland Street, on to Park Street, Camden Town, close to main entrance.

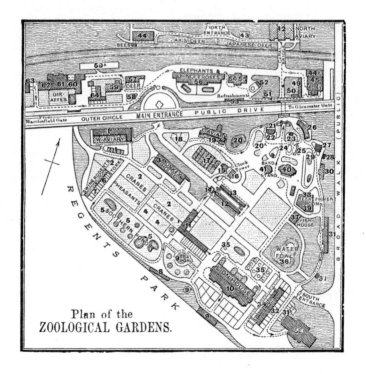

Plan of the
ZOOLOGICAL GARDENS.

SECTIONAL MAPS of LONDON

KEY TO THE FOLLOWING 15 SECTION MAPS

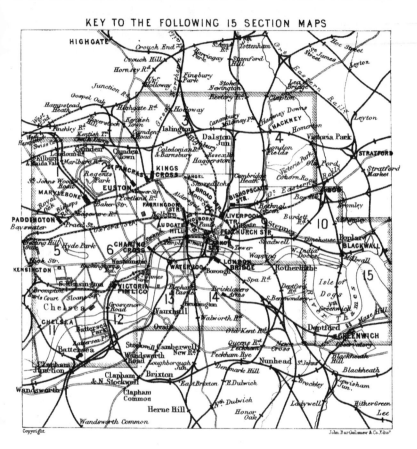

THE NEW LARGE MAP of the ENVIRONS OF LONDON
(14 to 20 Miles radius)
in colours showing Railways, Roads, Counties, &c., is at the end of the book.

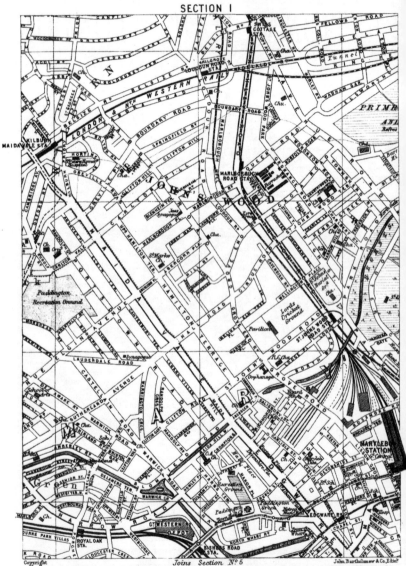

CHAS. BAKER & CO.'S STORES, Limited.—Edgware Road Branch of these Stores is
at 256 Edgware Road, corner of Chapel Street, close to the Metn. Railway Station.

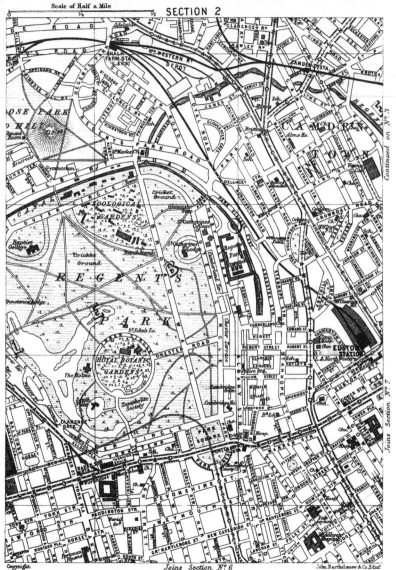

Scale of Half a Mile

Continued on N° 3

Joins Section N° 7

Joins Section N° 6

Copyright

John Bartholomew & Co. Edin.

THE TOTTENHAM COURT ROAD BRANCH of CHAS. BAKER & CO.'S STORES, now largely extended, is at the corner of Euston Road and at the end of Hampstead Road.

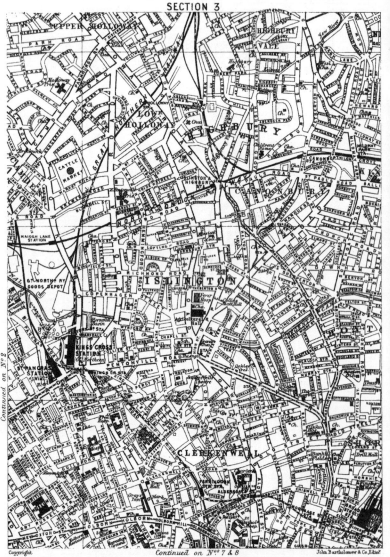

Continued on N° 2

Continued on N°s 7 & 8

Copyright.

John Bartholomew & Co. Edin.

CHAS. BAKER & CO.'S STORES, Limited.—LARGE EXTENSION OF HEAD DEPOT.—The Head Depot of the Co.'s Stores is 271, 272, 273, & 274 HIGH HOLBORN, next door to Inns of Court Hotel.

Scale of Half a Mile

Continued on Nᵒˢ 9 & 10

John Bartholomew & Co. Edinᵘ

Copyright

CHAS. BAKER & CO.'S STORES, Limited.—Clothing, Hosiery, Shirts, Hats, Boots, &c., at thoroughly moderate prices.—See Price List on pink pages at end of book.

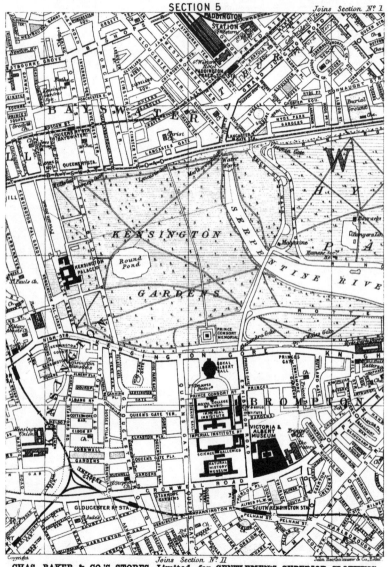

Joins Section No 2

Joins Section No 7

Joins Section No 13

Joins Section No 12

Scale of Half a Mile

Copyright

John Bartholomew & Co. Edinr

**EVERYTHING FOR GENTLEMEN'S & BOYS' WEAR supplied at
CHAS. BAKER & CO.'S STORES, Limited.**

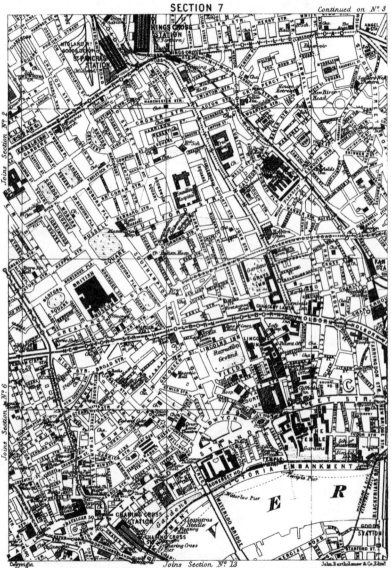

CHAS. BAKER & CO.'S HEAD DEPOT is at 271, 272, 273, & 274 HIGH HOLBORN, exactly opposite Red Lion Street and next door to the Inns of Court Hotel.

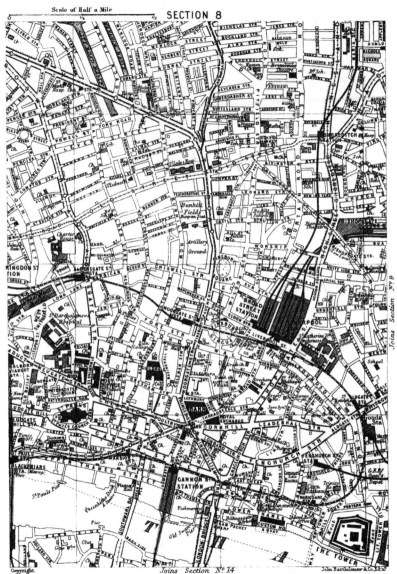

Scale of Half a Mile

SPECIAL NOTICE.—THE CITY BRANCH OF CHAS. BAKER & CO.'S STORES, Limited,
is at 41 & 43 LUDGATE HILL, opposite Old Bailey.

Copyright.

John Bartholomew & Co. Ld.²

Joins Section No. 14

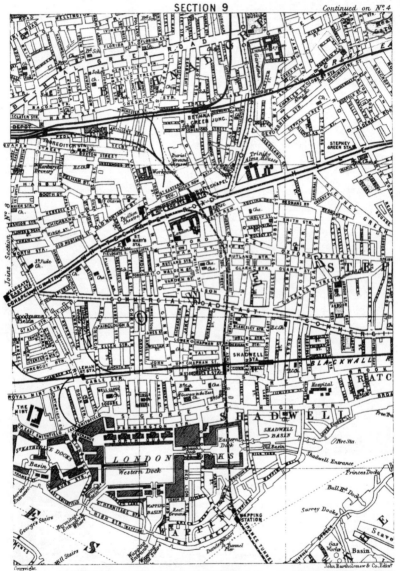

Scale of Half a Mile

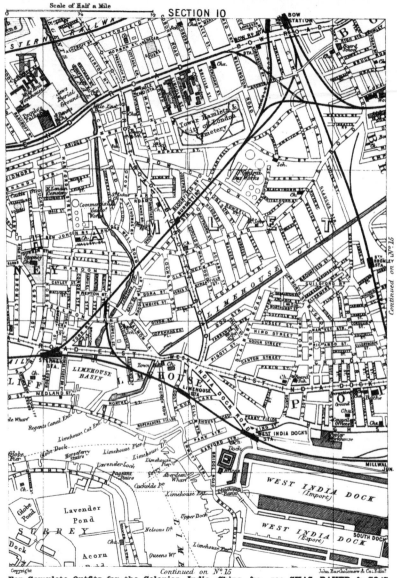

Continued on Nº 15

Continued on Nº 15

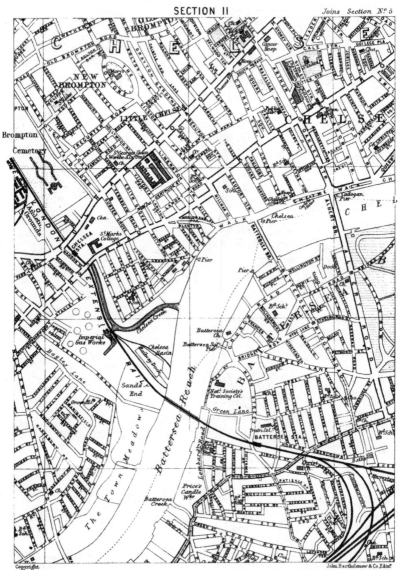

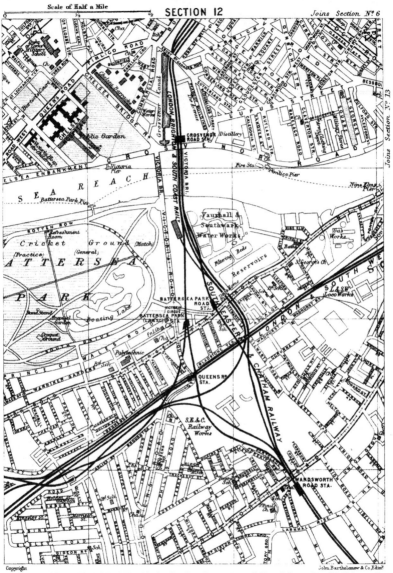

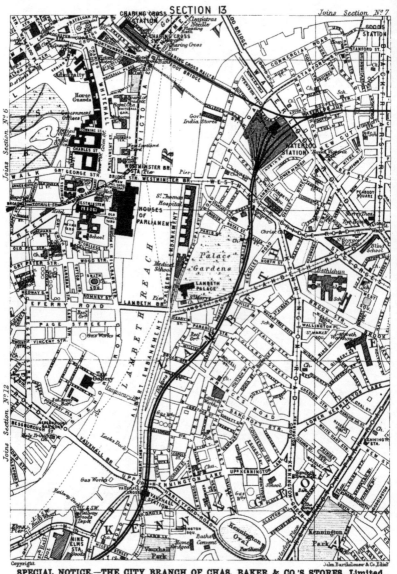

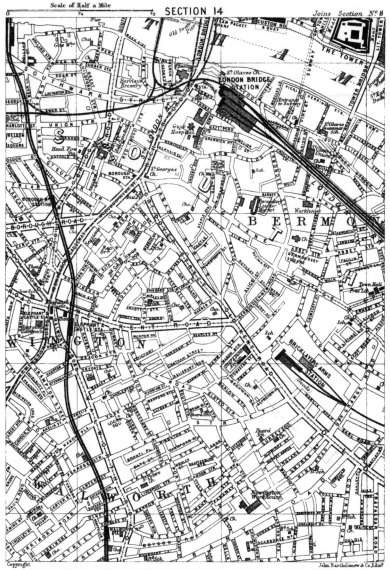

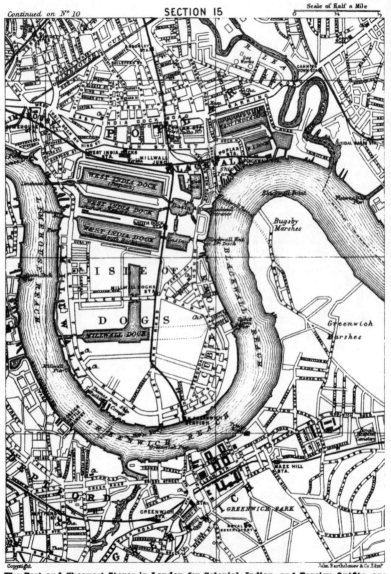

CHAS. BAKER & CO.'S STORES LIMITED.

HEAD DEPOT.

Hammersmith & North London Branches

CHAS. BAKER & Co.'s PRICE LIST.

GENTLEMEN'S FROCK COATS and VESTS

IN SUPERIOR BLACK CHEVIOTS, VICUNAS, etc.

READY FOR IMMEDIATE WEAR:
29/6 39/6
49/6 59/6

TO MEASURE:
39/6   43/6
49/6   59/6
64/6

5

6

CHAS. BAKER & Co.'s PRICE LIST.

GENTLEMEN'S
MORNING COATS
and
VESTS

IN BLACK SERGES, CHEVIOTS, ETC.,
For BUSINESS WEAR.

READY FOR IMMEDIATE WEAR :

19/11	24/6
29/6	34/6
39/6	49/6

TO MEASURE :

29/6	32/6
35/6	39/6
44/6	49/6
54/6	

7

CHAS. BAKER & Co.'s PRICE LIST.

CENTRAL LONDON ADDRESSES:

—

271, 272, 273 & 274,
HIGH HOLBORN.

—

41 & 43,
LUDGATE HILL.

—

137, 138, 139 & 140,
TOTTENHAM COURT ROAD.

—

256,
EDGWARE ROAD.
Etc., Etc.

GENTLEMEN'S

DRESS SUITS

TO MEASURE
In Fine Twills,

55/6	59/6
67/6	74/6
79/6 to	99/6

—

ALSO READY FOR
IMMEDIATE WEAR:

49/6 69/6

89/6

8

CHAS. BAKER & Co.'s PRICE LIST.

CENTRAL LONDON ADDRESSES :

271, 272, 273 & 274,
HIGH HOLBORN.

41 & 43,
LUDGATE HILL.

137, 138, 139 & 140,
TOTTENHAM COURT ROAD.

256,
EDGWARE ROAD.
Etc., Etc.

GENTLEMEN'S
JACKETS
and
VESTS

In Black Serges and Cheviots.

Ready for Immediate Wear :

14/11	16/11
19/11	24/6
29/6	34/6
39/6	

To Measure:

27/6	33/6
37/6	39/6
44/6	49/6

9

CHAS. BAKER & Co.'s PRICE LIST.

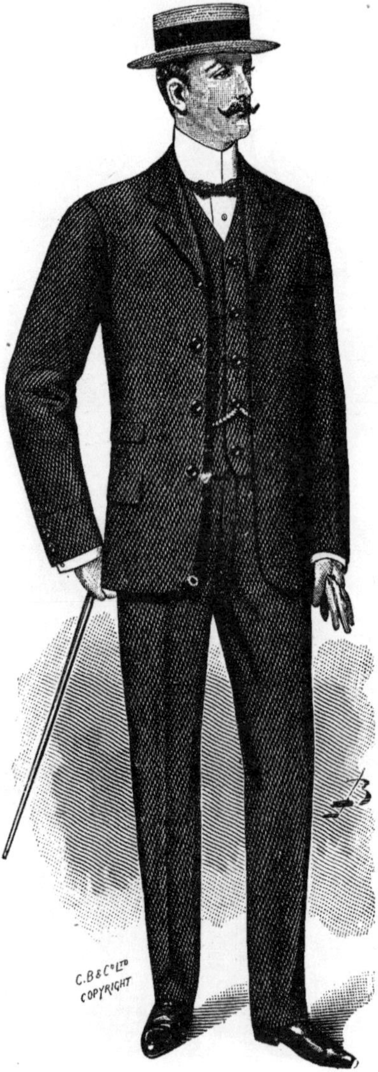

10

C.B & Cᵒ LTD
COPYRIGHT

GENTLEMEN'S
SERGE SUITS
(Blue or Black).

READY FOR
IMMEDIATE WEAR:

21/- 24/6
29/6 34/6
39/6 49/6
59/6

TO MEASURE:

35/6	39/6
42/6	47/6
52/6	59/6
69/6	

PATTERNS
POST FREE.

CHAS. BAKER & Co.'s PRICE LIST.

GENTLEMEN'S TWEED SUITS

READY FOR IMMEDIATE WEAR:

21/-	24/6
29/6	34/6
39/6	49/6
59/6	

—

TO MEASURE:

35/6	39/6
42/6	47/6
52/6	59/6
	69/6

C.B & Cº LTD COPYRIGHT

11

CHAS. BAKER & Co.'s PRICE LIST.

12

Gentlemen's Overcoats

—

Chas. Baker & Co. have always a splendid assortment of Overcoats. This illustration shows a Winter Overcoat made up in medium or heavy weight Cheviot or Vicuna. On the other side is shown a light texture Overcoat for Spring or Autumn wear.

—

READY FOR
IMMEDIATE WEAR:

16/11	19/11
24/6	29/6
39/6	49/6
59/6	

—

TO MEASURE:

29/6	34/6
39/6	49/6
59/6	69/6

CHAS. BAKER & Co.'s PRICE LIST.

Light Texture Overcoats

In Tweeds and Worsteds.

READY FOR
IMMEDIATE WEAR:

19/11	24/6
29/6	39/6

Silk-Lined **49/6**

TO MEASURE:

29/6	34/6
39/6	44/6
49/6	54/6

13

CHAS. BAKER & Co.'s PRICE LIST.

NORFOLK SUIT

READY FOR IMMEDIATE WEAR.

FOR TOURING AND CYCLING.

In Tweeds & Cheviots.

Jacket and Knicker-bockers.

—

Ready for
Immediate Wear.

29/6, 39/6, 49/6.

To Measure.

**34/6, 39/6, 47/3
52/6, 55/6.**

Patterns Post Free.

—

CENTRAL LONDON ADDRESSES:

—

271, 272, 273 & 274,
HIGH HOLBORN.

—

41 & 43,
LUDGATE HILL.

—

137, 138, 139 & 140,
TOTTENHAM COURT ROAD.

—

256,
EDGWARE ROAD.

Etc., Etc.

15

16

TROUSERS READY FOR IMMEDIATE WEAR.

In Good Quality Tweeds and Cashmeres,

BEST VALUE, STYLE, AND LARGEST SELECTION IN LONDON.

4/11, 5/11, 6/11, 8/11, 10/9, 12/11, 14/11, 16/11, 18/11.

To Measure in the Best Cashmeres, Tweeds, etc.

10/6, 12/6, 14/11, 16/11, 18/11, 21/-, 22/6.

NOTICE. — THE PRICES AND ILLUSTRATIONS ON THE PREVIOUS PAGES ARE ONLY RE-PRESENTATIVE OF THE LEADING AND MOST POPULAR STYLES IN GENTLEMEN'S CLOTHING. **CHAS. BAKER & CO.'S COMPLETE PRICE LIST,** including **LIVERIES, etc.,** **FORWARDED POST FREE** on application.

LITTLE BOYS' SUITS
CHAS. BAKER & Co., LTD.

LITTLE BOYS' CONWAY SUIT.
Jacket and Knickers.
In Blue Serges, with White or Coloured Collar
and Vest. Also in Fancy Cloths.
6/11   8/11   12/11   15/9   19/11   24/6

LITTLE BOYS' CLYDE SUIT.
Made up in Fine Cloths of various colours.
6/11   8/11   11/9   15/9   19/11
The newest Style of Children's Costume.

BOYS' SAILOR SUITS

As supplied at Chas. Baker & Co.'s Stores, Ltd.

ROYAL NAVY SUITS.
In Blue Serges, Complete,
4/11, 6/11, 8/11, 11/9,
14/11, 18/11, 21/6.
Regulation Straw Hats,
1/11, 2/11, 4/11.

MIDDY SUITS.
In Superfine Blue Cloth,
Ready for immediate wear,
43/6 to 49/6.
To Measure,
49/6 to 59/6.

MAN-OF-WAR SUITS.
In Blue Serges,
7/11, 9/11, 14/11, 21/6.

Sailor Caps,
1/-, 1/6, 2/6, 3/6.

BLUE SERGE KNICKERBOCKERS, 1/11, 2/11, 3/11, 4/11 per pair.

BUCKINGHAM SUIT.
Jacket, Vest and Knickers,
5/11,   7/11,   8/11,   12/11.
In Superior Tweeds and Serges,
15/9,   18/11,   22/6,   25/9,
Boys' Tweed and Serge Knickerbockers,
1/11,   2/11,   3/6,   3/11,   4/11.

NORFOLK SUIT.
Jacket and Knickers, in Durable Tweeds
and Cheviots.
4/11,   5/11,   8/11,   11/9,   14/11.
Very Superior,
16/11,   19/11,   24/6.

RUGBY SUIT.
Jacket, Vest and Knickers in Good Durable
Tweeds,

7/11,   9/11,   11/9,   14/11,   17/9,   22/6.
In Real West of England Cloths, 25/9, 29/6.
In Black or Blue Serge,
7/11 9/11 11/9 14/11 17/9 22/6 25/9 29/6.
Prices quoted for Boys of 12 Years.

SUFFOLK.
In Scotch and Irish Tweeds and Cheviots,
without Vest,
12/11,   16/11.
With Vest, 16/11, 19/11, 22/6, 24/6, 27/6.
A Strong School Suit.

Chas. Baker & Co.

Makers of   Ltd.,

SCHOOL CLOTHING

FROM MATERIALS SPECIALLY SELECTED TO RESIST HARD WEAR.

The Prices of SCHOOL OUTFITS, complete with a full list of articles required, are given in

CHAS. BAKER & CO.'S ILLUSTRATED PRICE LIST.

Eton Jacket and Vest.

For Boys from 9 years of age. Ready for immediate wear. Thoroughly well cut and made. In Vicunas and Fine Worsted Cloths.

Range 1 ... **15/9 to 18/11**	}	according
Range 2 ... **17/9 to 25/9**		to
Range 3 ... **22/6 to 31/6**		Size.
Range 4 ... **27/6 to 39/6**		

Eton Jackets and Vests to Measure,
21/6 to 27/6, 25/6 to 33/9, &c.
Patterns Post Free.

Hairline Trousers, 4/11 to 5/11.
5/11 to 7/11, 6/11 to 8/11, 8/11 to 10/9,
9/11 to 12/11, 10/9 to 14/11,
11/9 to 16/11,
According to Size.

CHAS. BAKER & Co.'s PRICE LIST.

BOYS' AND YOUTHS' CRICKET, TENNIS AND BOATING OUTFITS.

25 PER CENT. UNDER USUAL LONDON PRICES.

Fig. 2.   Fig. 3.

White Flannel Knickers,	Boys',	$\left\{\begin{array}{l}\text{2/11 to 3/11}\\ \text{3/11 to 5/11}\end{array}\right\}$	Youths', 5/11, 6/11.
White Flannel Trousers,	Boys',		Youths', 4/11, 5/11, 7/11.
White Flannel Shirts,	Boys', 2/11, 3/11, 4/11		Youths', 3/6, 4/6, 5/6.
Blue Flannel Jackets,	Boys', 2/11, 3/6, 3/11, 4/6		Youths', 5/11, 6/11.

FLANNEL SUITS (as Fig. 3).
Jacket and Trousers only, Boys' and Youths', 15/9 to 19/11.

23

Youths' Suits

MANUFACTURED BY

CHAS. BAKER & CO.

In the Latest Designs of Tweeds and Cheviots,

10/9   12/11   14/11   16/11   19/11   25/9.

In real West of England Cloths, in Scotch and Irish Tweeds,

29/6   35/6   41/6.

In Blue Serges, Rough Cheviot or Fine Twill,

At similar prices to above.

Also in Black Cheviots,

10/9   12/11   16/11   21/6   25/9   29/6   35/6   41/6.

CHAS. BAKER & Co.'s PRICE LIST.

YOUTHS' SUITS.

25 PER CENT. UNDER USUAL LONDON PRICES.

YOUTHS' TWEED SUITS.

With double breasted Vest in very superior qualities,

27/6,   29/6,   31/6,   35/6.

YOUTHS' JACKETS AND VESTS.

In Black Serges and Vicuna Cloths,

10/9,   12/11,   16/11,   19/11,
24/6,   27/6,   33/9.

YOUTHS' TROUSERS.

4/11,   5/11,   6/11,   7/11,   8/11,
9/11,   10/9,   12/11,   and 14/11.

Chas. Baker & Co.'s

WINTER
OVERCOATS

FOR

BOYS AND YOUTHS.

BOYS' CHESTERFIELD

as illustration, for Boys 7 to 12
years of age,

6/11 7/11 9/11 11/9
13/9 15/9 18/11 22/6.

Youths'
Chesterfield Overcoat.

In the New Fancy Tweeds and Scotch
Cheviots, made in the Latest Style.

7/11 9/11 11/9 13/9
15/9 18/11 22/6 26/9
31/6.

The Fashionable Rough Tweeds in
Light Colours are made up in Boys'
and Youths' Overcoats, and range
from 11/9 upwards, according to
size and quality.

These Overcoats are
Chas. BAKER & Co.'s
own Manufacture.

CHILDREN'S ✿
FANCY
OVERCOATS

In Great Variety.

BOYS' NORTHCOTE OVERCOAT.

Made up in Tweeds and Covert Coatings.
Specially designed for boys of 5 to 10
years of age.

9/11   13/9   16/11

**THE
HOWE OVERCOAT.**

The latest for Boys of 3 to 10 years.
Made up in Blue Serge and plain
Blue Cloth, also in coloured Venetians
with collars to match.

6/11,   8/11,   11/9,   15/9,   19/11,
24/6

27

Chas. Baker & Co.'s Price List.

HOSIERY and UNDERCLOTHING.

Gentlemen's Half-Hose.

Unbleached Cotton ...	-/6½	-/9½	1/-
Fine Cotton (Dressed) ...	...	...	1/-
Fancy Striped Cotton ...	...	-/9½	1/-
Ditto extra quality ...	...	...	1/6
Summer Merino, in Drab and Fawn	-/6½	-/9½	1/-
Ditto extra quality ...	...	1/6	1/11
Natural Wool ...	-/9½	1/-	1/6	1/11
Black Cashmere, with Embroidered Fronts ...	...	1/-	1/6	1/11
Worsted...	...	1/-	1/6	1/11
Scotch Lambswool ...	...	...	1/-	1/6
Heavy Shooting Socks ...	...	...	2/6
Spun Silk Half-Hose ...	...	3/11	4/11

Gentlemen's Hose.

Unbleached Cotton...	-/6½	-/9½	1/-	
Merino	...	1/6	2/-	2/6
Worsted ...	1/-	1/6	2/-	2/6
Scotch Lambswool ...	...	1/6	1/11	
Shooting and Golf Hose—				
1/11 2/6 2/11 3/11 4/11				

Gentlemen's Underclothing.

	VESTS. Chest Measures.			PANTS. Waist Measures.		
	34 in.	36 in.	40 in.	34 in.	36 in.	40 in.
Summer Merino	2/11	2/11	3/6	3/6	3/6	3/11
	4/11	4/11	5/6	5/6	5/6	6/6
White Mer. (Smmr.Wght.)	3/6	3/6	4/6	4/6	4/6	5/6
	4/6	4/6	5/6	5/6	5/6	6/6
Shetland Merino	1/11	1/11	2/6	1/11	1/11	2/6
	2/11	2/11	3/6	2/11	2/11	3/11
	3/11	3/11	4/6	3/11	3/11	4/6
	4/11	4/11	5/6	4/11	4/11	5/6
NaturalUndyed Wool (Smmr.Wght.)	2/6	2/6	2/1〔	2/11	2/11	3/11
	3/11	3/11	4/6	4/11	4/11	5/6
	5/6	5/6	6/6	6/6	6/6	7/6
NaturalUndyed Wool Winter Wght.	4/6	4/6	4/11	4/11	4/11	5/6
	5/11	6/11	6/11	6/11	6/11	7/11
	7/11	7/11	8/11	8/11	8/11	9/11
Silk ...	7/11	8/11	9/11	8/11	9/11	10/9
	10/9	11/9	12/11	12/11	13/9	15/9
	15/9	18/11	22/6	18/11	21/9	24/6
	22/6	24/6	28/9	24/6	26/9	31/6

Ladies' Hosiery.

Ladies' Black Cotton Hose	1/-	1/6

Ladies' Black Cashmere Hose—

Plain ...	1/-	1/6	1/11	2/11	3/11
Ribbed ...	1/-	1/6	1/11	2/6	2/11

Ladies' Black Spun Silk Hose—

1/11	2/11	3/11	4/11	5/11

Ladies' Silk Embroidered Hose—

In Black or Colours	8/11	10/9	12/11

Boys' Hosiery.

To match Knickerbocker Suits, in Black and Navy Blue Cashmere—

1/- to 1/4   1/3 to 1/9   1/9 to 2/3

Heavy Knicker or Bicycle Hose, in Black, Navy or Heather—

1/6 to 2/4   and   1/11 to 2/8

Boys' Half-Hose—

Merino -/9½ 1/- 1/6, Worsted 1/6 1/11

Children's Three-quarter-Hose—

1/2 to 1/8

Gentlemen's Collars.

Polo Shape ...	3/6 per doz.
Military ...	4/6 ,,

All the Newest Styles of the Season.

6/- and 7/6 per doz.

Boys' Collars.

Eton Shape, 4/6 and 7/6 per doz.

Gentlemen's Ties and Scarfs, &c.

In the largest variety, 6½d., 1/-, 1/6, 1/11. 2/11.

Gentlemen's Gloves.

2-Button Cape, 2/6, 3/6, 3/11.

Boys' Calf Gloves, 1/11, 2/6.

Braces.

6d., 1/-, 1/6, 2/-

Chas. Baker & Co.'s Price List.

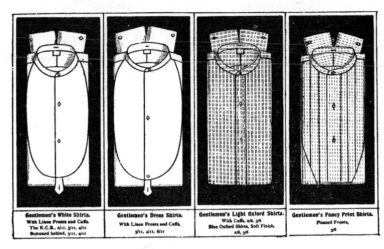

Gentlemen's White Shirts.
With Linen Fronts and Cuffs.
The K.C.B., 2/11, 3/11, 4/11
Buttoned behind, 3/11, 4/11

Gentlemen's Dress Shirts.
With Linen Fronts and Cuffs.
3/11, 4/11, 6/11

Gentlemen's Light Oxford Shirts.
With Cuffs, 2/6, 3/6
Blue Oxford Shirts, Soft Finish.
2/6, 3/6

Gentlemen's Fancy Print Shirts.
Pleated Fronts,
3/6

GENTLEMEN'S & BOYS' SHIRTS

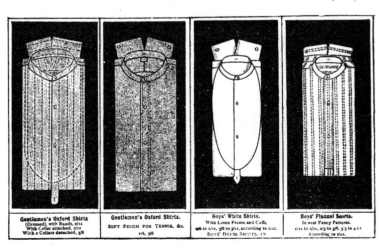

Gentlemen's Oxford Shirts.
(Dressed), with Bands, 2/11
With Collar attached, 2/11
With 2 Collars detached, 3/6

Gentlemen's Oxford Shirts.
SOFT FINISH FOR TENNIS, &c.
2/6, 3/6

Boys' White Shirts.
With Linen Fronts and Cuffs.
2/6 to 2/11, 3/6 to 3/11, according to size.
BOYS' DRESS SHIRTS, 4/6

Boys' Flannel Shirts.
In neat Fancy Patterns.
1/11 to 2/11, 2/3 to 3/6, 3/3 to 4/11
According to size.

25 per cent. under usual London Prices.

GENTLEMEN'S FELT HATS.
1/11, 2/11, 3/11, 4/11, 5/11, 6/11, 8/11.
In Colours,
3/11, 5/11, 6/11.

GENTLEMEN'S SOFT FELT HATS.
Black, 2/11, 3/11, 5/11, 6/11.
In Brown and Drabs,
(11.

Gentlemen's Silk and Felt Hats.

GENTLEMEN'S SILK HATS.
In the latest London shapes.
7/6, 8/11, 10/6, 12/6, 14/6, 16/6, 18/6.

CHAS. BAKER & Co.'s STORES, LTD.

GENTLEMEN'S STRAW HATS.
1/11 2/6, 4/11, 6/6.
Fancy Bands, -/6½, 1/-

BOYS' AND YOUTHS' STRAW HATS.
White or Speckled, 1/-, 1/11, 2/6, 3/6.

GOLF CAPS.
In Tweeds, -/6½, 1/-, 1/6, 2/6.
In Harris Tweeds, 1/11, 2/6, 3/6.

PANAMAS IN GREAT VARIETY.

COMPLETE PRICE LIST POST FREE.

LITTLE BOYS' DEESIDE CAPS.

In Tweeds, 1/11, 2/11, 3/11.
In all Fancy Shades, 1/3, 1/11, 2/11, 3/11

MAN-OF-WAR CAPS.

In fine Blue Cloth, with name
on band, 1/-, 1/6, 2/6, 3/6.

Embroidered front, with badge,
1/11, 3/6

BOYS'

HATS

AND

CAPS.

BOYS' SILK HATS.

For Wear with Eton Suit, &c.
6/11, 8/11, 10/6.

CHAS.
BAKER
& Co.'s
STORES,
LTD.

LITTLE BOYS' ALPINE HATS.

In Black and Brown Felt,
1/11, 2/6, 3/6, 4/11.
Light Colours, 2/6, 3/6, 4/11.

BOYS' AND YOUTHS' FELT HATS.

In Newest Shapes.
1/11, 2/6, 3/6, 4/11, 6/11.

Chas. Baker & Cos.'
SPECIAL LACE AND BUTTON BOOTS

FOR

GENTLEMEN.

No. 2.
GENTLEMEN'S LACE BOOTS.
Willow or Brown Calf, Stout Sole.
12/11, 14/11, 16/11
Hand-sewn, 18/11, 21/-

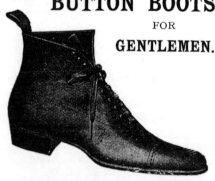

No. 1.
GENTLEMEN'S LACE BOOTS.
Calf Goloshed, Kid Leg.
6/11, 8/11, 10/9, 12/11, 14/11.
Hand-sewn, 16/11, 18/11, 21/-

No. 7.
GENTS' CALF SHOES.
6/11, 8/11, 10/9, 12/11.
Extra Qualities, Hand-sewn,
14/11, 16/11.

No. 3.
GENTLEMEN'S BUTTON BOOTS.
Calf Goloshed, Kid Leg,
10/9, 12/11, 14/11, 16/11.
Hand-sewn, 18/11, 21/-
Glace Kid, 10/9, 12/11, 16/11, 18/11, 22/6

No. 8.
GENTS' TAN SHOES.
6/11, 7/11, 8/11, 10/9, 12/11.
Extra Qualities, Hand-sewn,
14/11, 16/11.

LADIES' & CHILDREN'S BOOTS & SHOES.

LADIES' GLACE KID SHOES.
6/11, 8/11, 10/9, 12/11,
14/11.

❧

*Complete
Price Lists
forwarded
Post Free
on
application*

LADIES' BOOTS.
Kid, 5/11, 8/11, 10/9, 12/11.
Kid, Calf Goloshed,
8/11, 10/9, 12/11, 14/11, 16/11.
Glacé Kid, 16/11, 18/11.
Glove Kid, 18/11.
Tan Boots, 10/9, 14/11.

LADIES' GLACE KID BOOTS.
Button or Laced, 8/11, 10/9,
12/11, 14/11, 16/11, 18/11.

BOYS' PATENT SHOES.
4/3 to 6/11.
According to size.

LADIES' TAN SHOES.
Calf or Glace.
6/11, 8/11, 10/9, 12/11, 14/11.

BOYS' CALF SHOES.
5/6 to 7/3, 7/3 to 9/3.
According to Size.

BOYS' SCHOOL BOOTS.
For Hard Wear, 4/9 to 6/6,
5/11 to 7/11, 8/- to 10/-
Hand Sewn, 11/6 to 14/6.

(To face last pink page).